Heart Without Measure

Gurdjieff Work with Madame de Salzmann

Ravi Ravindra

MORNING LIGHT PRESS

MORNING LIGHT
P R E S S

Morning Light Press
323 North First, Suite 203
Sandpoint, ID   83864

www.morninglightpress.com

First published by Shaila Press 1999
Revised paperback edition published by Morning Light Press 2004
Copyright © 1999, 2004 by Ravi Ravindra

Cover photograph of Madame de Salzmann, New York 1990 © David Sailors

Printed on acid-free paper in Canada.
ISBN: 1-59675-000-6
LCC: 2004016996
SAN: 255-3252

These recollections are dedicated to
Madame Jeanne de Salzmann with love
and with gratitude for embodying a
heart without measure.

Preface

It has been gratifying to note that, in spite of the very restricted distribution of *Heart Without Measure* since its publication nearly five years ago, so many people in the groups connected with the Gurdjieff Work as well as those not involved in the Work have been nourished by the material. The book has been translated into Portuguese, Spanish and French by people dedicated to the Work. Some searchers have wished to make a connection with the Gurdjieff Work after reading this book. Several people who were close to Madame de Salzmann and had heard her over many years have said that they could hear her voice here. The publishers have received many notes of heartfelt thanks for the publication of *Heart Without Measure*.

We have decided that this material should now be available for a wider distribution. We had great hesitation in publishing this book initially and would not have done so without the encouragement and the support of Dr. Michel de Salzmann, Madame de Salzmann's son, who became responsible for the Gurdjieff Work after her death. The content in *Heart Without Measure* is very subtle in nature and can be easily misunderstood or misappropriated. The insights and remarks of Madame de Salzmann can be used as slogans if they are repeated without a corresponding practice being undertaken. However, it has been always clear to me that the work of Madame de Salzmann brought a fresh and strong light to the remarkable teaching of Gurdjieff and that she would not have spent such a large amount of time and energy with me as she did simply for my sake. She had asked me to write about the Work, and it is a necessity laid upon my soul. I have an obligation to make her teaching available to those who can benefit from it.

More and more I see the need for staying in front of the lack, recognizing the gap between what one knows and what one is. More and more I see the need for persisting in practice in order to understand the extraordinary teaching brought by Madame de Salzmann.

A few minor changes have been made for this edition to add clarity and to remove some personal details.

Man has a special function, which other creatures cannot fulfill. He can serve the earth by becoming a bridge for certain higher energies. Without this the earth cannot live properly. But man, as he is by nature, is not complete. In order to fulfill his proper function he needs to develop. There is a part in him which is unsatisfied by his life. Through religious or spiritual traditions he may become aware what this part needs.

— *Jeanne de Salzmann*

Contents

Introduction

Madame Jeanne de Salzmann was given the responsibility for the Work by Gurdjieff before his death in 1949. She fulfilled her obligations with an extraordinary intelligence and force until her death in 1990 at the age of one hundred and one. Among other things, she was responsible for the publication of the books by Gurdjieff, for the production of several films of the Movements and of the film, *Meetings with Remarkable Men*, directed by Peter Brook. She guided the establishment of the Gurdjieff foundations in Paris, London and New York. Her main contribution, however, was the bringing of many pupils to a new level of understanding.

My own contact with the Work was through Mrs. Louise Welch, whom I met in New York in 1968. She became my mentor in the Work and soon after, my spiritual mother. She herself had been a pupil of A.R. Orage in the twenties and later of Gurdjieff and Madame de Salzmann. Mrs. Welch took me to see a Movements class at the Gurdjieff Foundation in New York in 1971. After the class she introduced me to Madame de Salzmann. Almost a decade later Mrs. Welch recommended I work with Madame de Salzmann, to whom she wrote on my behalf. I went to see her in Paris in February 1980. I had seen Madame de Salzmann occasionally in the Work groups in New York and had met with her individually a few times during the previous several years. Over the following decade, however, I met her many times, both privately and in the Work groups, mostly in Paris, sometimes in New York and occasionally in London. It was not easy to be in her presence; with her,

1

more than anywhere else, I often felt my nothingness, but I never felt diminished. On the contrary, she always evoked inspiration and hope. Her being called me towards an authentic existence and demonstrated its possibility.

In 1986, after the death of J. Krishnamurti, I had written a small piece based on journal entries of my meetings with him. Mrs. Welch liked it very much and she wondered if I could write something about Madame de Salzmann. I was quite resistant to this task, if for no other reason than the fact that my journals contained far more entries about meetings with Madame de Salzmann than with Krishnamurti. However, whether to write or not to write about my work with Madame de Salzmann did not seem to be a matter of personal choice. I started assembling all of my journal entries in which Madame de Salzmann was mentioned. At the end of 1986 I was able to send to Dr. and Mrs. Welch all the relevant entries. They were very interested in the notes I had sent them and encouraged me to continue.

The material gathered here is based on journal entries over a period of twenty years, from 1971 to 1990. These entries were not intended for publication or for perusal by anybody other than myself. Often in very abbreviated or mnemonic form, they were meant to be reminders to myself of what had struck me at various times and places, sometimes in a state of consciousness clearer than my usual state. The entries concerning the meetings with Madame de Salzmann are scattered among jottings on various topics, including ancient Sanskrit verses from the Vedas and exercises dealing with the intricacies of French grammar, or impressions of the awesome cathedral at Chartres and of subjective negative reactions to someone or something. I began editing and combining the notes from several entries in order to remove excessively personal details and to gather a few coherent recollections which might be read aloud. Dr. Welch first read some of these notes in the Gurdjieff Foundation in New York in 1990. He telephoned me with the encouraging report that some people thought these notes were translations from Madame de Salzmann notebooks.

What is presented here is essentially the way it was in my journals. Although a strict chronological order has not been maintained, there is a more or less historical sequence. The dates and places of the journal entries, which in general coincide with the dates and places of the meetings, are indicated at the end of each section. I have tried to be faithful to a logic of feeling rather than of grammar and syntax. The interest here is less in putting the words of Madame de Salzmann into correct or elegant English but more in maintaining her voice.

The recollections reported here are not based on tape recordings. Therefore one cannot be certain, except in the case of a few letters in her own hand, that these are the precise words of Madame de Salzmann. What we have here is how the mind and heart of one of her many pupils resonated to what he heard in her presence. All the journal entries were made as soon after the meeting as possible, sometimes within a few minutes of the meeting, but sometimes with a delay of as much as a day. There is also the caveat that what was said was meant only for that occasion and for the person who was there and may not have general applicability. Readers will have to decide what is relevant to their own situation.

Many of these recollections have been read by senior people in the Work, some of whom had heard Madame de Salzmann over many decades and had worked with her very closely. Their responses have been reassuring. I wish to express a special gratitude to Dr. Michel de Salzmann for carefully reading the manuscript and making numerous helpful suggestions. However, the sole responsibility for the presentation of everything included here is mine. It is to be expected that different pupils would have been differently struck by the extraordinary presence and teaching of Madame de Salzmann, and in conveying their impressions, each one would naturally emphasize what was most significant and helpful to them.

It is hoped that some readers will find nourishment here for their search. A spiritual path is more like a footpath than a highway. Unless enough wayfarers tread the path, it will become overgrown with brush and weeds and will be lost to future pilgrims. This journal account is offered to all those searchers who feel obliged to help keep the path open.

Of course, there was much which cannot be recounted here simply because it is too personal or intimate or likely to be misunderstood without a great deal of explanation.

It will be obvious from these recollections that Madame de Salzmann was most generous with her time, energy and attention. There could not be anything personal in this. Any serious spiritual work is neither the teacher's nor the student's; it is always an objective work in which they both participate. Naturally, it expresses itself through the particular make-up of the teacher and of the student, but the search is always towards a clarity of perception so that subjective energies and talents might serve what is real.

What Do You Serve?

Something had been churning inside me for a long time. I had been feeling that I was getting old and that I could no longer postpone engaging with what is real. Mrs. Welch suggested that I work with Madame de Salzmann and, having written to her on my behalf, she advised me to go to Paris as soon as I could arrange it.

I arrived in Paris at the end of February 1980 and a time was arranged for me to see Madame de Salzmann at six o'clock one evening. I wanted to be early so that I would not arrive agitated and rushed. I left the cathedral of Notre Dame de Paris about four-thirty in the afternoon, assuming that I would arrive for the appointment by about five-fifteen and have plenty of time for collecting myself.

It is amazing how little we know about the forces which resist and oppose whatever we undertake. Perhaps anything serious must have a serious opposition at its own level. For me, meeting Madame de Salzmann was serious.

I still do not know exactly what happened, but there I was in the Metro and the train would not move. People all around me were getting agitated and talking more and more loudly. Not knowing any French did not help. I had no idea what was going on. I asked several people; finally someone said in English that there was some trouble on the line. Everyone assumed that the train would soon leave. Much time passed and there was more and more agitation. Many people left the train— in order to travel by other means, I supposed. I tried to determine the nature and gravity of the problem and to weigh my options. Someone said in English that a member of the Metro workers' union had been killed, probably in front of a train, and that the workers had gone on an impromptu strike. By this time it was a quarter to six and my appointment was at six o'clock.

Finally, still quite uncertain about the most efficient course of action, I left the train, hoping to catch a taxi. Outside, there had been a sudden storm. It was raining heavily and everyone was looking for a taxi. Having wasted a lot of time trying to stop one, I started walking, then running. I was not familiar with the city and was very uncertain how far I had to run. I ran for about half an hour before I succeeded in hailing a taxi. Even with all my good intentions, I arrived at the door of Madame de Salzmann's apartment almost an hour late, out of breath, drenched and thoroughly chagrined. Her daughter-in-law opened the door and was furious at me for keeping Madame de Salzmann waiting. She said that Madame had a meeting to go to and probably could not see me now. Still, she went inside to check.

Soon, Madame de Salzmann came out herself. She was completely calm and collected and took me into the living room. I was anxious to explain and to tell her that it was not my fault that I was late, that there were circumstances beyond my control, and so on. Before I could say anything at all, she said, "It is important not to give in to reaction. I have a meeting very soon; but I shall see you. They can wait."

I wondered about the insight she had, and about the level and perspective from where she saw the world and myself. The meeting lasted for half an hour or a little longer, and she stressed the need for working. She asked me how I work and with whom. She advised me to come to Paris for a longer time: "Come when you can, and for as long as possible." I said I could arrange to come in a few months. She said that would be a good time, but that I should write ahead or telephone.

As I was leaving, she said to me that I should come with her to the Maison, as the house of the Work is called in Paris, and afterwards her chauffeur would drive me where I had to go. Being driven in a comfortable car to Notre Dame, where I was going to meet the rest of my party, along the roads where an hour earlier I had been running in the rain trying to catch a cab, seemed quite ironic. Earlier, I had been beside myself with frustration and helplessness. Now, again I was almost beside myself with the anticipation of a new direction to my life.

❖ ❖ ❖

The next day, a person who commutes from London once a week to come to the meetings in Paris thanked me for delaying Madame de Salzmann for his meeting. Apparently, the same sudden rainstorm had delayed his flight from London and he would have missed the meeting if she had arrived on time. He thanked me with much sincerity and conviction as if I had delayed her intentionally and especially for his sake.

He saw the whole thing from his point of view, as I did from mine. Madame de Salzmann had a much larger perspective.

❖ ❖ ❖

On another occasion, there was a feeling of great substance and profundity in the exchange at a group meeting with Madame de Salzmann. What she said did not affect me as much for the ideas as physically, as if what she said had a measurable weight. Her words seemed to be a continuation of the music played earlier in the evening, which had set my whole torso vibrating with an intense feeling. Her presence had a glow; I wondered if this is what is meant by a halo in religious literature.

Someone had asked a question in the meeting: "How do I know that I am here for a purpose? It may be so, but it is not my experience. Similarly with many other ideas in the Work. To me, the human position is ultimately absurd. A person may give meaning to his life, but there is no higher meaning in it."

This was so peculiarly my own question that it seemed contrived for my sake. It was asked with genuine sincerity, without showing off and without sentimentality. Madame de Salzmann's answer did not register with me for its ideas; it was just music. All I remember is her saying, "You don't love yourself enough, the Self that needs and wishes to emerge." She spoke for about fifteen minutes. It was like the sound of very fine crystal.

I have rarely been quieter and lighter than I was during that meeting. There were two very strong impressions: she was so much more visible than the other people sitting close to her; secondly, for a moment I felt as if she, as a whole and not only her voice, was inside me.

In a meeting a few weeks later I described to Madame de Salzmann the experience of feeling her inside me. She said, "That was an example of real listening. In an experience like that we do become each other although we are still separate." Generally, this sort of statement does violence to my reason, and to my notions of space and time. I asked her, "In the face of an obvious violation of spatial relations, reason balks. What check is there against imagination?"

She said, "You want to know all these things with your head because you trust it more than anything else."

"Why do I want to make a theory of it?" I asked. "Why does my head do it? I don't want it to."

She smiled and then said, "If I tell you now, it will satisfy your head and you will think you understand, when in fact you don't."

Before she had come in, I had asked myself, "What would you want to ask of the wisest person in the world?" Somehow, any question seemed beside the point. Understanding is so clearly a matter of slow, methodical work that just asking a question means nothing. Besides, what would one pay for the answer, with what kind of currency?

❖ ❖ ❖

I have just returned from spending about half an hour with Madame de Salzmann. As I think about it, I feel rather terrified: it cannot be that one can be given so much without something being demanded as payment, sooner or later. I feel so full and uplifted in her presence. It does not seem to matter what question I ask, or whether I even ask a question.

Her mere presence blesses me. How does one pay for her generous gifts of time, attention and energy?

I asked how to hear and to see. I said I do not see others or even myself as really human and alive. I seem to be isolated from everyone and blind to everything. The reason for this seemed to me to be self-occupation, which strikes me as almost the essence of being satanic.

She said, "You are prepared, and you should make more and more demands on yourself. You need to have someone near you who can help. But you must also give. In calling others to work, your own work is deepened. But above all, you must feel the need to know yourself. You are something and you don't know it. You have to acknowledge that you do not know who you are, and that you need to know it. This opening is the most important step.

"You can read in Hinduism or Buddhism what this opening means; or you can read it in Mr. Gurdjieff's books. It is the same thing. There are different levels of energy. And one can sometimes be in a truer current.

"You need a knowledge which is not a book knowledge. Then the head can be informed by reading books where you recognize your experiences. What is needed is direct perception.

"Movements will help you. In the Movements, the important thing is not the positions, but the impulse, the energy, from one posture to another. And nobody can teach that; you have to watch it within yourself."

❖ ❖ ❖

When I next went to see Madame de Salzmann, she asked what I was working on. I did not know. I suppose the fact is that I am not working on any damn thing. If I am sincere with myself, I have to say that I just dream, and sometimes dream of working.

She said, "You see this side, the mechanical side, and you know that something exists on the other side. What can make the connection between the two? Sometimes it is possible to place oneself in the middle."

She reiterated the need for an inner connection between the centers; not only as an idea but in experience. I have heard her say this before, but it struck me freshly. In my case, I occasionally see the absence of this connection but not its presence.

Madame de Salzmann said to the group at lunchtime, "What do you serve? There is something in you—a higher energy—which is worthy of respect. Without this you serve only your pleasures. This is not to say that you should not look after the needs of the body or of the mind. Unless you respect and serve the finer energy in you—which is not you—work here has no sense."

New York, 1971-76; Paris, February 1980.

Stay in Front

I had phoned Michel de Salzmann from Canada asking his advice about which dates to come to Paris. I said that my intention was to stay a month unless he advised otherwise. He said, "You are big enough to know what you want. You decide what you want, then try it. If there is resistance, you adjust."

I pondered a long time about what I wanted, but I was not clear. What is my aspiration? I wish to know if there is a purpose for my existence here on the Earth, to know what is demanded of me, and to try to carry it out. One thing which is becoming quite clear is that I need to change radically, to undergo *metanoia*, to turn inward to what is real and essential. At what stage of life am I too old to take the world so seriously?

❖ ❖ ❖

My arrival in Paris was just about as badly timed as it could be. Because of the religious holidays everything was closed, including the Maison. I began to feel quite sorry for myself because of my bad luck. But it is amazing how little one knows what is really good for oneself. It seems difficult to allow the forces to help. I always interfere, thinking that I know better. In actual fact, the holidays turned out to be very helpful: I was able to see Madame de Salzmann right away since she was not as busy as usual with meetings and other activities at the Maison.

Madame de Salzmann seemed pleased about the effort I had made in just going there and in trying to learn some French. She was interested in the fact that before coming to see her I had gone to the Alliance Française and registered myself for four hours of French every day. She said, "I see how you do things!" Now that she knew that I could not speak French, she said that I could ask questions in English.

Three days after arriving in Paris I received a telegram sent by Madame de Salzmann to me in Canada and redirected from there. It said, "If you don't speak French it will be difficult. Come for a few days and see. Affectionately, Jeanne de Salzmann." It was just as well that I did not get this telegram before I left.

I had come to Paris with all sorts of reservations. People in New York had said that the French are not at all warm to foreigners. That has not been my experience; nor had it been so on the previous visits. I have been given much more than I had dared hope or imagine. Madame de Salzmann recommended I participate in everything—Movements classes, group meetings, meditation sittings. She suggested that I meet with all the senior people in the Work. In addition, she wanted to see me herself, often.

I had lunch with Madame de Salzmann and Michel the next day. I was struck by the fact that she ate very lightly. We talked about many things, including Krishnamurti, whom she much appreciated and whom she regarded as an exceptional human being. I told her that Krishnamurti was too much of a saint for me. I said that what interested me about the Gurdjieff teaching was the inclusion of everything—even the Devil is there.

There is something so entirely sane, normal and lovable about Madame de Salzmann. She is overflowing with love, but there is nothing sentimental in this. She has an enormous common sense and makes room for everything and everybody—in their right place. By contrast, Krishnamurti—clearly a person of very high being—seemed to be so correct, so good, almost pious. There is such a partiality in his insistence that process must be excluded, that traditions are only traps, that thought at all levels breeds fear, that one must not have anything to do "with money, sex and all that." I told Madame de Salzmann about a conversation I had had with Krishnamurti. I had said to him that just as a diver needs to be loaded with some heavy material to go lower down in the ocean, he should put on a belt of lead in order to come down to our level; otherwise, he is too light and cannot be in contact with the Earth, where we are. He asked me, "What do you mean, sir? What kind of belt?" I replied, "Krishnaji ... a little meat and sex."

He found it amusing, but refused to engage with the idea, and said, "Sir, you are too clever for your own good."

Madame de Salzmann was characteristically generous: "You can see the inner freedom Krishnamurti has. But he does not have a science of being; Mr. Gurdjieff brought a science of being."

While Madame de Salzmann was sitting there, Michel said, "As far as I am concerned the best advice I can give you is to stay in my mother's *darshana* as much as possible." I was struck by his use of this Sanskrit word, commonly used and understood in India; he was advising me to remain in her sight and presence, to abide near her.

After lunch, Madame de Salzmann and Michel lit up cigarettes. She offered me one, but I said I did not smoke. She asked me, with the most wicked and mischievous smile, "And, *monsieur*, what is your weakness?"

I must have had a holier-than-thou sentiment in my refusal of the cigarette. Her smile would have undone the most pious saint. I laughed and asked if I should catalogue my sins! It was good-hearted banter. I offered to do anything around the place—dishes, or typing, or whatever was needed. Michel said he would find something.

Later, when I was back at the place where I was staying, I resolved to smoke occasionally. However much I detest smoking, I am sure that being a pious prig is worse.

Madame de Salzmann asked what I was working on. She had asked this earlier too. I said that I tried to watch my breathing, and also to do some breathing exercises regularly. She asked me to show her these exercises. I did so. When I asked her about the desirability of continuing these exercises, she said, "They will not get you far. But they will do no harm. If you find them useful, do them."

I told her that I wish to understand the great ideas of the Work concretely. I know of them, but I do not know the reality behind them directly. I said, somewhat to my own surprise, "*Je ne les connais pas directement, immediatement.*" (I do not know them directly, immediately.)

I told her that sometimes in teaching or in groups, I come alive and that I am often surprised by what I say. She said, "It is necessary to have that relationship. In that situation it makes connection for you.

"Ideas are necessary. Mr. Gurdjieff worked on ideas for years with Ouspensky. Then he shifted to direct work, and Ouspensky wanted ideas and explanations which Gurdjieff refused. In part that is why Ouspensky left. It is necessary now to work directly on matching the head and the body."

This is something she has been emphasizing and I must try to understand it in experience. She said, "I cannot do it, but I have to try. If a connection is not made, stay in front of the lack of connection. It is necessary to know this lack. I cannot do it, but it can be done in me; and I have a part to play.

"The Earth is in exchange with higher levels of existence. For this an apparatus is needed. Mankind is that apparatus. This exchange is not automatic; it requires work."

❖ ❖ ❖

In a group meeting Madame de Salzmann placed a great deal of emphasis on active participation. This struck me as very important. I see I have enormous passivity. I act as if I have no real responsibility for my own evolution, as if it were a matter of grace which I am somehow guaranteed. She said that Mr. Gurdjieff brought a science of being, but I see that something in me does not accept the fact that there are exact laws of spiritual evolution. I keep dreaming and hoping that the law will not apply to me, that I will win a spiritual lottery and wake up a higher being.

❖ ❖ ❖

I have a recurring image of Madame de Salzmann, exhorting, questioning. Is it my own conscience? Alter ego? Apart from a clearer sensation in the body, it seems that nothing changes, nothing happens, nothing gets done. I pass most of my life as if in a haze in which nothing is clear and nobody is distinct. It is as if I am not alive to anything or anyone, not even to myself. I have a definite feeling that nothing would change in me even if someone very close to me were to die. No doubt, I would be hurt; I would express grief and the like, but there would be no radical change. The point is that in death or in life, in failure or in success, I do not feel really alive and present to the moment. I am not connected to what is taking place. It is as if all this is happening to someone else. The fact that I am a dying creature—slowly but inevitably dying—does not seem to make an impression on me. I am like a man drunk, passing through a scene in which someone cries for help, and the man momentarily stops, following some reflex, and stares at the source of the sound, uncomprehending. Then he stays there or moves along, not knowing what he is doing or why.

It seems that I have no idea how to make an effort. All I learn from any effort is that I cannot make an effort. I act as though it would be very nice if someone else would take command of and responsibility for my life. Who would? Why? Besides, would I let anyone? Can I follow instructions? Can I obey? Will I let anything disturb my comfort?

❖ ❖ ❖

During a group meeting in New York, Madame de Salzmann asked why I was not speaking. I said—and I had thought about it already, it was pre-formulated—that whenever she spoke it was all clear, but later, when I was alone, nothing was clear. Everyone laughed, and she said it was not completely true. She said, making a gesture with the whole body, this way or that way I always get out. Mrs. Welch then said I was very clever. After a pause, Mrs. Welch said, as if to everyone, "Speak now. If you dare you can perhaps find something about your chief feature."

I had a sense there was something I could see; but I did not see it clearly. Perhaps only this: somehow I manage to wiggle my way out of every situation—with words and ideas—so that I can avoid seeing. There is a fear of seeing the truth about myself.

❖ ❖ ❖

Madame de Salzmann laid much stress on attention. Attention is all that we have; that is to say, attention is all that we can bring. The rest is out of our control. The demand that we need to make is that of attention. We need not only to pay attention but also to pay with attention.

Madame de Salzmann reiterated the need to make a connection between the centers, not only as an idea but in experience. She said, "Even with a fine mind and a sensitive body, and very good instincts, you need a connection between the head and the body. Neither one should be stronger than the other. They have to have equal force. Then feeling will arise.

"Try for some time. Stay in front of the fact that you are not connected. Try again after three or four hours. Will and active initiative are needed."

I said I sometimes feel the need for an external force; as if I need someone else to discipline me forcibly.

She said, "If necessary, set yourself some punishment, or deprive yourself of some pleasure."

I have sometimes thought about punishing the body or depriving it of some pleasure, but something in me manages to justify not doing it. I see that there is enormous possibility for self-deception and self-justification, arising from constant dreaming. I need to struggle against my passivity—both of the mind and of the body—and remember her instruction: "Stay in front of the fact that you are not connected. Will and active initiative are needed."

New York, 1973-79; Halifax, March 1980; Paris, May 1980.

What Is Your Question Now?

Madame de Salzmann said, "I am very happy that you have come. You must keep in contact. Meet all the leaders here. They emphasize different things, things that have helped them. Perhaps you will come here for a longer time and work on something with them. You would especially understand Henri Tracol and Michel. I would ask you to do something, like speaking to groups, but language is the problem at present."

There is a strong feeling in me that this is the right moment for me to have come to Paris. I am fed up with my usual self, which just daydreams and wants to be important. I asked Madame de Salzmann, "Why do I need to be important? I see it is stupid and useless, but I carry on."

She said, "We wish to have an action on others around us—a real action. But when we are not related with higher energy and cannot have a real action, we try to have other kinds of action, so that we will not be pushed around."

What she said made much sense to me and it clarified many things. I saw that I try to be important externally—by pretending, by boasting or even by a show of humility—when I am not strong inside or connected with anything real.

I told Madame de Salzmann that although I do not wish to be passive, I don't want to have too many plans and schemes of my own, and that I wish to be available to what she suggests. She wondered if I should go to London with her when she goes there in a couple of weeks.

Meanwhile, she suggested that I should meet with all the principal leaders and go to Movements with all three of the main teachers—Josée de Salzmann, Pauline de Dampierre and Marthe de Gaigneron. "Tell them I have sent you. Movements will be good for you."

I told her, "I feel I am too old for the Movements. Even more generally, I sometimes feel that I am too old now to come to anything real. I feel that it is too late."

"No", she said, "it is not too late for you."

She said that we should work together a little before I go to the groups. Then she led me in a meditation. When there was some quiet and an internal connection in me, she said, "Without man the Earth cannot receive the energy from a higher level. So, if some people work consciously, they assist the descent of this energy. Otherwise, there is discord on the Earth. One can sense it."

This struck me as a very interesting way of putting the ancient idea, present in so many great traditions, that human beings are especially responsible for the maintenance or re-establishment of cosmic harmony, and that without their conscious participation there will be disorder in the universe.

She said, "It is important to bring the body and the mind—a different mind, not the usual mind—to the same rate of vibration. Then there is a relationship, as between a man and a woman, and a child can be produced—a new feeling. Higher energy is there, but we do not receive it because we are fragmented. The purpose of man's existence on the Earth is to allow the exchange of energy between the Earth and higher levels of existence. That is not possible without the relationship between the body and the mind."

She must have sensed in me a certain hankering for a monastic life and some ascetic tendencies. Without my saying anything, she added, "Not that a man should not have a woman, or not eat, or do other things. One need not change what one is. But what is this for? All this, all of one's life and activities, are not for oneself, but for something else. They are for the sake of the higher energy."

I wondered to myself if this sense of service to the higher energy is what motivates the senior people in the Work. This made much more sense to me than working for the sake of developing 'individuality' or gaining 'immortality'.

I have had a long-standing question about the relationship between the strength needed for action in the world and the lightness necessary for contacting the spiritual realm. In practice, in general, I am pulled either one way or the other. Somewhere I understand the need for balancing the two. I believe it was Meister Eckhart who said, "What we receive in contemplation we give out in love."

❖ ❖ ❖

In another meeting Madame de Salzmann asked, "What is your question now?" I saw how heavy I was, that I had not worked, and that I was not interested. I had just been sleeping—literally and figuratively. It is clearly important to know what I am working on. She has often said that one needs to try something all the time. She had once said to me that intentional suffering was bearing the indifference of the pupils to the work and their lack of understanding, and still not losing hope. I felt now that I was adding to her suffering. I experienced remorse of conscience. For some reason I recalled the saying of the Christ that if a fig tree does not bear fruit it will be cut down. Then I was seized by an unknown terror.

Even remorse and terror do not seem to bring about any real change in me. I know that I must work. I understand this, but I do not act on that knowledge. What level of seeing and suffering is required for that knowledge to have an action on me, immediately and deeply?

Madame de Salzmann said, "What you try in sensation is superficial. It needs to go deeper. Try for two hours or the whole morning, when doing anything, to keep an eye on yourself and to have deep sensation. Perhaps this is what you try, but you need more intensity. You must have other people to work with. At that time, when teaching and working with others, you come to something, some relationship with higher energy."

She emphasized the need of not being soft on oneself. She said, "Sometimes Mr. Gurdjieff was really hard on people. He would tell them: *'Vous merde; et pas seulement merde, mais mousse de merde.'* But, after a little while, he would say in a completely different tone, *'Oh, très honoré, Mister Merde ...'* You could not stay angry with him.

"Make a demand upon yourself. If you don't come to something when you try, punish yourself. Deprive yourself of what you like. But have patience. Don't get angry at yourself and beat yourself. Not to try all at once, but slowly, steadily. All the time, try something. There is deep passivity. You must see this and struggle against it."

Paris, May 1980.

Why Am I Here?

I arrived at the Maison for what was supposed to be a men's group at seven o'clock, to which I had been invited by Madame de Salzmann. There seemed to be either no such group or it was meeting somewhere else. Somehow whatever happens always turns out to be useful. All the confusion about the place and time of the meeting of the group had a fortunate result for me: a private meeting with Madame de Salzmann. I do not really understand these things but I feel that there must be a guardian angel taking care of me.

We walked together to her house from the Maison. On the way, since it was almost dinner time, I suggested that we go out for dinner. She seemed a little surprised, but found the suggestion agreeable. "That would be very fine. But if I go out with you, it will cause a reaction in some people. They would say, 'Why him? Why not me?'" I was struck by the weight of responsibility she carries. Unless done intentionally, a teacher cannot be partial, or favour one pupil over another. And at our usual level, we live in reaction and always view everything partially and personally. Part of the suffering of the teacher must be the stupidity and reaction of the pupils.

At her house, she asked me to show her how I usually sit for meditation. I sat in the full lotus position on the floor. She said it was fine, but not sufficient by itself. I told her of my efforts to sit longer, or otherwise to make the body uncomfortable from the very start by taking some awkward posture, so that I would be forced to struggle with myself.

She said, "It is right to try many things so that one can know directly what will help. The kind of relationship with the body which is needed is not with the muscles of the body. The mind—the higher mind, literally on the top of the brain—needs to have its energy relate with the energy of the body. For that, one needs an attention which is quicker than the usual mind. The ordinary mind is too slow and is not able to make the connection. One can see that very well in the Movements.

"Don't change anything. You cannot change anything. Notice that you are unrelated, fragmented. That attention—and staying in front of the lack—will allow a connection to be made. Higher energy cannot be forced. What is at your command a little is your attention. Just watch the body and the mind with an attention which is quicker than both. Have patience. Try this several times a day. Not for long at any time, just fifteen minutes."

She advised against torturing the body; that would produce a wrong relationship. If one notices something which is bad or harmful for the body or the mind—something which makes one dull or less sensitive—one naturally stops, as one naturally refrains from eating poisonous substances.

❖ ❖ ❖

Last evening at the Maison, I looked for Madame de Salzmann since we had agreed to meet there. She looked very tired and said that since I was going to Holland with Michel later that evening we did not need to meet now. I said that I had been looking forward to being with her, and that I needed it. She said, "Well, come with me." We returned to her home and worked there for some time. My soul was much nourished. I see the importance of wishing to work and of having some persistence. A master can never refuse to meet a student's real need. Of course, no true teacher wishes to squander time and energy simply out of sentimentality. Unfortunately, their energy may still be wasted if the student does not respond to the teacher's efforts made in hope.

Madame de Salzmann very much emphasized—as she has often done—the need for an integration of the mind and the body before one can be related to anything higher. She underscored the necessity of keeping a deep sensation of the body. She spoke about the exercise of sensing the limbs and saying "Lord, have mercy." "Maybe Mr. Gurdjieff brought it for the people in the West. You can say the words which touch you. This exercise can help."

She suggested that for the next two or three days I work on this exercise, and on the relationship between the body and the mind. "Then we shall speak further about the next step. Right now, this is the most important thing. At least half of your attention should be on it all the time."

I see more and more the need for making one's inquiry organic, and not merely mental.

I have been amazed by the persistence and depth of tensions— the physical ones and even more so the emotional ones. It is almost as if what I call myself is essentially a ball of tensions. The more I see, the subtler the tensions I discover. I remember hearing Madame de Salzmann say that one can be free of tensions only at a very high level. Below, there is always some tension, and also some fear.

Madame de Salzmann said, "At this stage you don't need ideas; you need facts. What you know directly is a fact."

She has been very much emphasizing the need for a connection between the mind and the body. Feeling will come automatically as a result of the union of these two, as a child is born from the union of a man and a woman.

While working with Madame de Salzmann I was much more related with myself and with something higher. The sad fact is that in general this fine energy is there, going to waste, unrelated with the body where it can be useful. It is as if the angels are crying in the wilderness of myself, and I do not answer.

She asked me to try to see her every day while I am in Paris. How does one understand the demand created by this generosity? What am I going to give in return?

❖ ❖ ❖

Madame de Salzmann seems to begin every time from the beginning. And what she says seems so clear as she speaks. "Man has a special function, which other creatures cannot fulfill. He can serve the Earth by becoming a bridge for certain higher energies. Without this the Earth cannot live properly. But man, as he is by nature, is not complete. In order to fulfill his proper function he needs to develop. There is a part in him which is unsatisfied by his life. Through religious or spiritual traditions he may become aware what this part needs.

"The whole universe is made up of forces and energies. They have to be in relationship with one another. The Earth has its own level of energy; it needs human beings for the purposes of right relationship with other energies. This is what man is meant to serve.

"To be able to bring higher energy in contact with the Earth, man must have a harmonious relationship—a right exchange—among his centers. Everything is in movement. The energies of our centers are in movement too, but not in harmony with each other.

"You need to learn how to work. One succeeds more or less, but it must be clear what is to be done. Work with others, often. Even for a few minutes. That will help you very much.

"Mind and body both have resistance. You need to understand that. You must ask repeatedly, 'Who am I?' and 'Why am I here?'"

Paris, May 1981.

Your Body Is Not Only Yours

I had not had a meeting with Madame de Salzmann for two days. I was struck by the fact that I missed her—in an organic way, as one wants something to drink when one is thirsty. When I saw her next I told her that I had missed her. She was very interested in what I had to say. She asked me to try to understand what it is that one misses. She said, "What you say is true. At the Prieuré, sometimes we met Mr. Gurdjieff in the morning and then he would go away to Paris for the afternoon. When he would come back we realized that we had missed him. One misses what one needs. It is a food."

❖ ❖ ❖

Madame de Salzmann makes a clear distinction between 'thought' and 'associations'. Thought has direction and action; associations merely turn in reaction, but have no action. What I ordinarily call thoughts are only accidental associations.

In response to a question of mine, Madame de Salzmann said, "Watching the breathing can help in deepening and maintaining sensation. That is how one becomes aware of the energy of the body.

"Make a demand on yourself. If you do not succeed in making a connection, deprive the body of what it likes."

I told her about my reaction to seeing myself fragmented and dispersed. Sometimes I suffer the fact that I am in pieces. But often I am amused, as if I am watching a monkey in a circus, or someone else in a play. Somehow, the latter is also a form of suffering, and I think it is less personal and freer. She said that although both are certainly there, suffering appears when one becomes serious.

I asked her about the traditional Indian and Christian writings which I find very engaging. She said, "Deep down they are all speaking about the same thing. But people who are talking about them do not understand them. You need to be in a special state in order to understand higher things. Religions have become partial and their real meaning has been lost. Mr. Gurdjieff brought an integral way of the mind, feeling and body, not emphasizing one more than the others."

In the groups Madame de Salzmann so much emphasizes the right bodily posture as a prerequisite for a higher quality of attention. At one moment, sitting very straight in her chair, she pointed to her foot and said, "If even a foot is not rightly aligned, the connection with the higher energy can be broken." She herself sits there like a stupa, demonstrating, by her presence, the right posture and the connection with the higher energy. I see more and more that posture is an essential part of the teaching. I felt that my body was too heavy and that I was not sensitive enough to see the harm done by the wrong placing of the foot. I suppose the body is like a musical instrument. A sensitive and accomplished musician is likely to be more aware of the various subtleties of the instrument than a novice. It seemed so clear that one needs to see a little before one can even realize the fact of one's blindness. Those who suffer for their fragmentation are already in purgatory; they may possibly hope for wholeness, for it is said that His Endlessness occasionally visits the aspiring souls in purgatory.

It struck me that the major difficulty lies precisely in this: one does not see that one is blind, and that it is possible to open one's eyes. It is absurd but true: it is difficult to accept that if my eyes were open, I would see what I do not ordinarily see. I see neither the terror of my present situation nor the wonder of what it could be. It is plain and obvious that as long as one is asleep, all progress is a dream.

❖ ❖ ❖

In another meeting Madame de Salzmann said, "Your body is not only yours."

I did not quite understand what she meant. But I have a sense that it is important, and that I need to understand her remark. I wondered what else, or who else, had a right to my body, or a stake in it? What does my body serve? Only myself? What do I serve? I was convinced that her remark was intimately related with her earlier advice to me: "Ask yourself repeatedly, 'Who am I?' and 'Why am I here?' " I am sure it is like a Zen *koan* which I need to ponder deeply: Your body is not only yours.

Paris, May–June 1980.

One Cannot Behave Just Anyhow

I had heard from an acquaintance that Gurdjieff's apartment on the *rue des Colonels Rénard* was being maintained by the Paris groups. I thought I should see it and asked Madame de Salzmann when I met her next. She fixed me with one of her penetrating gazes, which pierces not only the body but also the soul, and asked, "Why?"

I was undone. I was not at all prepared for her response. I imagined I was making a perfectly innocent and ordinary request. After all, why maintain the apartment if people in the Work cannot visit it? All kinds of chatter was going on in my mind. I was not quite sure what to say, or even in what direction to think. I was like an animal startled by sudden and glaring light, unable to move. As I was squirming inside, she asked again, with insistence, "Why?"

The whole episode did not last long by any objective measure, but it was long for me. I so much wished to withdraw my request. But now I was stuck with having to face myself. Why did I want to see the place? Why did I want to do anything? Was I meeting Madame de Salzmann for a casual chat? Was she spending her time and energy on me to satisfy my whims? It was clear that I had to answer her, and also that nothing could be hidden from her, even if I might try to hide it from myself.

Finally, I said, "I have no special reason for wanting to see the apartment. Until yesterday, I did not even know that it existed. It is mere curiosity on my part—at the same level as gossip." After a relatively long and uncomfortable pause, I added, "Also, I was hoping that I might have a special emotional experience there."

She smiled very warmly and said, "What you say is true. One wishes to get something without paying for it. Of course, you should see the place. It is important for you to see it. But you must see it in the right way, not anyhow. I will take you there myself. Come tomorrow! At ten."

I had no idea what had taken place. It seemed like the situation in so many mythological stories: the bumbling hero does not understand what he is doing or what he should be doing, but some fairy or maiden, or some animal, gives him just the right help through a hint or a word, and he succeeds in spite of himself. There was nothing serious or intelligent or earnest on my part, the sort of thing one might expect from a spiritual seeker, as I sometimes fancied myself. But there I was the next day, driving to Gurdjieff's apartment with Madame de Salzmann. I was no longer very eager to see the place, but now I was obliged. I could not go to see the apartment just anyhow, but I did not know how to contact another level of seeing.

Overnight I had tried to check out a detail which had flashed through my monkey mind, but I did not find the appropriate sources at that time. I recalled reading somewhere that for a little while, in the twenties, Krishnamurti had also lived on the same street. I mentioned this to Madame de Salzmann. She was interested and for a few moments we wondered if Krishnamurti and Gurdjieff had run into each other on the street. What would they say to each other? I told her about my impression that Krishnamurti was the most traditional anti-traditionalist whereas Gurdjieff seemed to me to be the most untraditional traditionalist. I was rather pleased with my clever formulation, and she even seemed a little amused. As the car turned a corner, suddenly she became silent, as if preparing herself for meeting someone in person.

The car stopped, and she led me upstairs in the building where the apartment is. She had to struggle with the keys and the locks to open the place. She took me to each room in turn, telling me about it in detail, and remarking disapprovingly about some of the changes which had been made. Many paintings and other things had been repaired or rearranged. The bedroom seemed to her to be the only room which was still more or less the way it used to be. In his private room, where he often met with people individually, books were now placed on the shelves where he used to have all sorts of food stuff. She was particularly concerned about the tendency among some people in the Work to project the 'right' image of Gurdjieff. At one point she said, "They want to put books there to make him look scholarly. Humph! What he had there was more interesting. He had real food!"

Reflecting on all this later, I realized how important it is to avoid moralism about the Work. 'I ought to do this' or 'I ought not to do that' always leads to a conflict of vice and virtue, or to an opposition between my freedom and an externally imposed discipline. We need to see what we are, what we lack, what we need. If we see, then we proceed from inside, seeking the conditions which help—as a plant naturally bends to get more light. The problem is not of ethics; one needs a science of being. We need to inquire in freedom. When we see the need for the right conditions, the need for help, for instruction, the need for other people, the need for payment, then we see that discipline and obedience sustain freedom and are not opposed to it. Then we see, from the inside, the need for discipline, or submission, the need for freedom not so much for oneself but from oneself.

If I inquire in freedom, I am in question. What am I? I see that I cannot do it, but without me it cannot be done. I cannot do it but in any case it has to be done, and I have a part to play. I can let it be done through me. The first renunciation is of inaction; the next one is that of egotistic action.

When we were in the living room of the apartment Madame de Salzmann asked me, "Shall we work for a little while?" We sat quietly for about fifteen minutes. Unlike her usual practice with me, she did not say anything or guide me in any obvious manner, but I was sustained and held by her presence.

Before we left, Madame de Salzmann said, "In Mr. Gurdjieff's presence one felt an extraordinary freedom to be what and how one wanted to be. He would give them food and drink—even oblige them to drink too much—to add to this freedom. But one could not behave just anyhow. One was always aware of a higher level in him."

Certainly, in the presence of Madame de Salzmann I have always felt an extraordinary freedom to be simply myself, without the burden of the usual considering, pretense and fear. However, being near a person of a higher level obliges one. It was clear that in front of her I could not behave just anyhow.

Paris, May 1980; Halifax, June 1980.

Right Alignment

You don't love yourself enough, the Self that needs and wishes to emerge.

❖

Above all, you must feel the need to know yourself. You are something and you don't know it. You have to acknowledge that you do not know who you are, and that you need to know it. This opening is the most important step.

❖

You need a knowledge which is not a book knowledge. Then the head can be informed by reading books where you recognize your experiences. What is needed is direct perception.

❖

You see this side, the mechanical side, and you know that something exists on the other side. What can make the connection between the two? Sometimes it is possible to place oneself in the middle.

❖

What do you serve? There is something in you—a higher energy—which is worthy of respect. Without this you serve only your pleasures. This is not to say that you should not look after the needs of the body or of the mind. Unless you respect and serve the finer energy in you—which is not you—work here has no sense.

I cannot do it, but I have to try. If a connection is not made, stay in front of the lack of connection. It is necessary to know this lack. I cannot do it, but it can be done in me; and I have a part to play.

❖

The Earth is in exchange with higher levels of existence. For this an apparatus is needed. Mankind is that apparatus. This exchange is not automatic; it requires work.

❖

You need to have a connection between the head and the body. Neither one should be stronger than the other. They have to have equal force. Then feeling will arise.

❖

Without man the Earth cannot receive the energy from a higher level. So, if some people work consciously, they assist the descent of this energy. Otherwise, there is discord on the Earth. One can sense it.

❖

It is important to bring the body and the mind—a different mind, not the usual mind—to the same rate of vibration. Then there is relationship, as between a man and a woman, and a child can be produced—a new feeling. Higher energy is there, but we do not receive it because we are fragmented. The purpose of man's existence on the Earth is to allow the exchange of energy between the Earth and higher levels of existence. That is not possible without the relationship between the body and the mind.

❖

Man has a special function, which other creatures cannot fulfill. He can serve the Earth by becoming a bridge for certain higher energies. Without this the

Earth cannot live properly. But man, as he is by nature, is not complete. In order to fulfill his proper function he needs to develop. There is a part in him which is unsatisfied by his life. Through religious or spiritual traditions he may become aware what this part needs.

❖

The whole universe is made up of forces and energies. They have to be in relationship with one another. The Earth has its own level of energy; it needs human beings for the purposes of right relationship with other energies. This is what man is meant to serve.

❖

To be able to bring higher energy in contact with the Earth, man must have a harmonious relationship—a right exchange—among his centers. Everything is in movement. The energies of our centers are in movement too, but not in harmony with each other.

❖

Mind and body both have resistance. You need to understand that. You must ask repeatedly, 'Who am I?' and 'Why am I here?'

❖

Make a demand on yourself. If you do not succeed in making a connection, deprive the body of what it likes.

❖

You need to be in a special state in order to understand higher things. Religions have become partial and their real meaning has been lost. Mr. Gurdjieff brought an integral way of the mind, feeling and body, not emphasizing one more than the others.

❖

If even a foot is not rightly aligned, the connection with the higher energy can be broken.

Did You Help?

ast evening I saw Peter Brook's film, *Meetings with Remarkable Men.*
This is the third time I have seen it. It is an entirely remarkable
film. I do not understand why I had reacted so strongly against it when
I saw it for the first time. What was I expecting? I felt that I should write
to Mrs. Welch apologizing, not as much for my negative reaction as for
my doubting and dismissing her when she said one has a different reaction to this film on seeing it the second and the third time. I had been
so sure about the objectivity of my reaction to it.

This film seems to me to be Madame de Salzmann's most public
statement about the Gurdjieff teaching. Perhaps it makes more sense to
me now since, being in Paris and in her presence so often for the past
three weeks, I feel I have been in a sort of monastery, as in the film.
Almost the same words have been said to me as to the seeker in the film,
and very similar situations of enhanced feeling have been present. After
all, it can hardly be a matter of some hidden knowledge in some far away
monastery. The knowledge is in fact hidden in the inaccessible places
in one's own heart. It is amazing how much preparation is needed and
how right the conditions have to be for one to make even an occasional
journey to inaccessible places.

Also, I was very struck by the fact that at the same place and the
same time, one might be a novice in the monastery or a tourist. Paris can
be the Sarmoung Monastery or it can be a tourist spot. It is easy to shift
from being a seeker to becoming a tourist, but it is not so easy the other
way around. I was obliged to ask myself, "What are you? A novice in the

monastery where there is much demand made on you? Or a tourist with no demands? What would you choose?"

❖ ❖ ❖

There was a grand and festive dinner at the de Salzmanns last evening. The conversation was a mixture of French and English. Feeling that very little time was left, I took the opportunity to speak to Madame de Salzmann before dinner.

She said, "Without the relationship with higher energy, life has no meaning. The higher energy is the permanent Self, but you have no connection with that. For that connection, a fine substance needs to be generated. Otherwise, the energy of the body is too low to make contact with the very high energy which comes from above. You must persist—stay in front of the lack. Gradually, arrange to be in conditions which help you.

"Slowly, the desire of the mind for that relationship will become an organic need. You cannot force it. Higher energy cannot be forced. If you try to force it, it can lead to bad results. Gradually, you get more and more interested in it, and appalled by the lack when you are not in relationship. It may be too early to use the word, but that is love. You come to a state in which you realize that you cannot live without that relationship. Nothing has significance or meaning without it.

"A group of people is needed for a certain level of energy to appear. You must work alone and also with other people—often."

As the time came to move to the dining table, Madame de Salzmann excused herself, saying something to the effect that she would leave the young people by themselves.

❖ ❖ ❖

Madame de Salzmann asked me whether I had found the meditation at the Maison last evening useful. She had not been feeling well and could not come herself. Someone else, a senior person in Paris, had led the meditation. I had felt a little disappointed by the fact that she had not come and I had not been able to make a deep connection with myself during the meditation. I made some complaint about the way the meditation had been led. Madame de Salzmann asked me something which struck me like a thunderbolt, and showed me the level of my self-occupation. She asked simply, "Did you help?"

It had not really occurred to me that I cannot simply be a consumer, that the Work is not all set up for me to get ahead spiritually, but that I have a part to play. It is not the responsibility only of the person leading the meditation to do a good job—on which I can then pass judgment. It is not only his search or his work. I also need to do my part in creating the atmosphere so that a connection with the higher energy may be possible for the whole assembled group. It is always possible to find fault. After Madame de Salzmann's remark it seemed so obvious that in any situation the only real and practical question is, 'Did I help?'

Paris, May 1980.

How Do You Work?

It was a very full day, with many activities. It is good to have this intensity. The sheer quantity of work may get through to me somehow, even if the quality of the effort I bring seems paltry.

Both in the morning at home and in the evening at the Maison, I made a special effort to prolong my cross-legged sitting for meditation. I experienced interesting sensations in the body and an unusual deepening of breathing. I can now sit for forty-five minutes. It is interesting that Dogen Zenzi thought that Zen is nothing but sitting rightly (*zazen*). I should work at extending my meditation to one hour. I can make at least this effort since I do not really understand what Madame de Salzmann means by bringing the mind and the body to the same strength in a relationship with one another.

Madame de Salzmann makes it clear that the function and purpose of a human being is to become a link, a conduit, for higher energy to come down to the Earth—to bring Heaven down to Earth. Our Father who is in Heaven may do His will here on Earth as He does in Heaven, but this is possible only if the River Ganga which flows in Heaven—above the head or on top of it—may flow down to the Earth, the body, and irrigate her.

The *Rig Veda* says we are children of Heaven and of Earth. Perhaps we have forgotten our connection with Heaven. Letting this energy descend into the body is to let Heaven come down to Earth. That is the incarnation of the Word.

Madame de Salzmann said, "Transformation is not a change of energy. You cannot change the higher energy. You can allow it to find a place in you. It is very difficult. It requires a lot."

❖ ❖ ❖

The work Sunday here in Paris is much the same for me as elsewhere. I always have a question about how to make physical work useful. The best part of the day for me was that I had a meeting with Madame de Salzmann. She is entirely remarkable. She exudes immense force, and really comes alive when she is working. With her around, all the others in the Work look so young.

When I am with Madame de Salzmann I feel convinced that the Work is the way for me to understand the real and my place in the cosmos, but when away from her, doubts return. Sometimes I think I am unnecessarily agitated about what the right path is for me. Whatever the path—perhaps destiny places one on any path—I need to work on it. To stop fighting fate and to accept one's destiny can be a relief. It can save a lot of energy which can then be used for needful action. Endless doubting is an escape from working. But one cannot be parochial about the Work. There seems to be a community of people, belonging to various teachings, who are attuned to the subtle vibration of Truth. Each one in this community has found certain forms or practices useful, but that need not prevent any of them from acknowledging the validity and efficacy of other ways. The Zen master, Roshi Kobori, when he discovered in a conversation that I knew Madame de Salzmann, had said, "She is the most remarkable woman I have ever met."

❖ ❖ ❖

My sister-in-law died yesterday. I see that I understand nothing about death, and very little about life. How can I help her in any way? When I try to sit quietly for a few minutes, my mind wanders. I cannot focus my attention. How could I help her or anybody else? How can I do anything? I see I have no control over, or even a relationship with, the energy that can be concentrated and focused and that can have an action. I see how the mind is taken by one thing or another, driven mostly by fantasy about this or that pleasure. Death and life; all this goes on, constantly. More than one hundred million people will die this year and the same number or even more will die next year, and more will be born. Mother Earth has an extremely destructive jaw and a very fecund womb. I, too, am on this conveyer belt, ineluctably moving towards death, all the while strutting, shouting to draw attention to myself, trying to make my little bargains.

I told Madame de Salzmann about my sister-in-law's death, about my total lack of understanding about death, and about my realization last night of my inability to help her. She said, "You cannot help her, because you cannot help yourself. You don't know how. To attempt to do what you cannot possibly do now is a waste of energy, and even harmful.

"There is an energy which is trying to evolve. That is why it comes into a body. If a person works and helps the evolution of this energy, at death this energy goes to a higher level. If one does not work, the energy returns to its own level. But the human life is wasted."

She so much emphasizes the need to understand the movement of energy and to sense the life we participate in. Not the ordinary life, but life within this life. As she said, "*Une autre vie dans la vie ordinaire.*" ("Another life within the ordinary life.")

❖ ❖ ❖

Madame de Salzmann keeps asking me, "How do you work? What do you actually do?" She really wishes me to taste something real and to be clear about what it means to work.

"Now, you don't need to read *Fragments*.* The important thing is to experience. If you wish, you may read something by Mr. Gurdjieff, where he answers pupils. But you must see your dispersion and fragmentation; you must see the need of the relationship of the mind with the body. The energy of the mind—of the higher part of the mind— must descend and embrace the energy of the body. Then something new will arise. You must suffer for your inadequacy. It is not easy. You have to stay in front of it. Without that, nothing is possible. One can use big words, read a hundred books and write a hundred books. It means nothing."

She wants me really to work and to know something, not only mentally, but in fact. I see the passivity of my body. She said, "Stay in front of your inability; that will change something. This relationship is the most important thing for you, of all the things you want. In the midst of everything else, come back to it. This is the most important thing: to stay in front of the lack, the inability.

"The whole work is about energies. One must understand the relationship of energies, inside oneself and outside in the groups. There is an exchange possible. That is what the work is about. You must work often during the day, with others and by yourself."

New York, 1973, 1979; Paris, May 1980.

Fragments is the short title of *Fragments d'un enseignement inconnu*, the French translation of P.D. Ouspensky's *In Search of the Miraculous: Fragments of an Unknown Teaching.*

Keep a Sensation
Throughout the Day

While engaged in meditation at home yesterday, I thought I heard someone—a French woman—call my name aloud three or four times from the street. The sound was distinct and strong. I got up and went to the window and said loudly, "Who is it?" No one answered. Clearly, it was not anyone. I was hearing something else; perhaps a deeper part of myself, a subconscious intimation. I wondered if Madame de Salzmann was reminding me of something during the sitting. Surely that is the time when I am much quieter and more connected inside than usual. At such times it is possible to be more receptive to subtler communication. Even when we meet face to face, first of all we work together quietly for twenty to thirty minutes so that I might become able to hear more subtly—so that I might hear behind the words, without argumentation and without the ceaseless chattering of the mind. In any case, I went back to my meditation. After finishing, I had breakfast. Something in me quite uncharacteristically wanted to sit in meditation again, and I did. I had an altogether new experience which left me feeling at the verge of something unexpected and momentous.

When I met Madame de Salzmann I reported to her the details of the unusual experience I had had. I also told her that a part of me was fascinated with extraordinary experiences, even though it is clear that one needs to be wary of seeking these or wishing to repeat such experiences. She said that was true; she seemed pleased and said that I had the beginning of an understanding.

Later, as we spoke together more casually, she wondered, apropos nothing that I was aware of, if I was familiar with Aikido. She thinks much of it; it was really useful for her grandchildren. She suggested that if there were a good Japanese teacher, I should study Aikido; perhaps my son too, if the teacher agrees.

In the general conversation about many things, I said that although Ouspensky seems so anxious in his books to be scientific, and not to be considered religious, he comes through to me as a religious ascetic. He seems to be so focused on the pure white light that he does not come through as permitting or enjoying the whole spectrum of color of human experience. She agreed that that was partly true.

I wondered about the unevenness of quality in the various chapters in *Beelzebub's Tales to His Grandson* and how I could be assisted in approaching it. She asked which chapters I found uneven. I said the "Ashiata Shiemash" chapters seem profound and deeply engaging; but chapters like "America" seem to me to be superficial.

She simply said, "Why write that?" Then she added, "That is what Ouspensky also wondered." Then she was quiet and did not say anything more. I did not press the point, for, naturally, my meetings with her were always on her terms.

❖ ❖ ❖

I was not feeling very well and arrived at the Maison for the meditation sitting rather tired. I decided to sit quite far back so that I would not disturb anyone. Madame de Salzmann remarked later that I must not be well, because she saw me restless in the sitting. Nothing escapes her!

Madame de Salzmann said to me, "You are working too hard. I can feel you. You look tired. Maybe you should have a day's rest. Your personality is like mine when I was young—determined." She made a gesture of approval, indicating recognition of strength, and expressing a slight bemusement, and continued, "Mr. Gurdjieff used to say, 'Ah!' "

Later she said, "I am going to London tomorrow. You stay here. If necessary, you can have me on the telephone in London."

When I said I did not expect to telephone her in London, she said very solicitously, "One never knows. Just in case it is necessary."

I did not know what trouble she was expecting me to get into. She had given me an exercise to work on and perhaps she wished to be certain that nothing untoward would happen in her absence. I was reassured by her concern.

❖ ❖ ❖

I discover deep-seated tensions in the body, as if every feeling and every thought leaves a corresponding mark. It is clear that the whole of one's life has to be understood and changed. To be really relaxed would be real freedom. I see clearly how low-level reactive emotions and thoughts produce tensions in the body, and that particular tensions correspond to specific negative emotions. It is also obvious that a certain kind of attention has an action on the body, transforming and regenerating it. Higher consciousness produces a new body; but equally, a new body is needed for connecting with higher consciousness.

❖ ❖ ❖

When I realize how much time Madame de Salzmann has spent with me, I wonder what is required of me. The Gospels say, "From him to whom much is given much is demanded." There is no question that much has been given to me. It cannot be only for my sake. My own self is too small to have any really worthwhile purpose of its own. It has to serve something higher. What is demanded? How can I understand this simply, without fantasy?

It seems that if one just waits, actively and intelligently, without being anxious, one receives much more than expected. How can one understand this? Are there forces—perhaps guardian angels interested in the welfare of the pupils—which help even when the pupils are not asking for anything definite? I was just sitting in the corridor at the Maison, trying to be present as best as I understand it, when Madame de Salzmann walked by. She stopped in front of me and said, "You wish to see me, perhaps?" What a question! But then, it was not really a question; it was more like a jug of water to a thirsty man.

She said, "The relationship between the mind—the higher mind— and the body is the most direct thing to work on. When these two energies come together, then something new will be born. This you must try every day. You will see many things—hidden tensions, hidden forces. We will not speak about that now. You will see. For that, sensation is useful. Keep a sensation throughout the day. Work with other people. They make you search more actively. When you know you need something more, come back. You can come anytime.

"More intensity and higher tempo are needed in the body, so that it will equal the mind in its force. Only then they can be related with each other."

Paris, May–June 1980.

Remorse and Affirmation

I was engaged by what Madame de Dampierre said to me about *Beelzebub's Tales to His Grandson*. She said, "What is important is what action something has on me; not whether it means this or that. Some people take the words in Beelzebub too seriously. Gurdjieff often made them up, so people would not have the usual associations. Sometimes he has a word which means 'god-god-god' using several languages, or 'duty-duty-duty'; and people read much into it."

It seems that no group in Paris is making a special study of *Beelzebub*, at least not at present, although there is a group studying *Fragments*. Madame de Dampierre said that the people in the group are asked to gather all their inner experiences connected with some important word or idea and to search for connections among them.

In speaking about the ideas, I said to her that it is obvious to me that one cannot understand great ideas with the lower mind. Yet, those who operate from the higher mind, such as Madame de Salzmann, do not seem to be interested in spending much time on speaking about the ideas. I had been struck by the remark of an ancient Sanskrit poet who claimed, "The scriptures are useless for those who do not know. And they are useless for those who do know. Therefore, the scriptures are useless!" Are ideas useless?

It is clear that scriptures and ideas are needed to focus the mind and to give it some direction. But it seems necessary to guard against fanaticism or exclusivism about any idea or expression. Surely, the vast reservoir of Truth cannot be exhausted by any form, however great. The bewildering array of gods, philosophies, cosmologies and mythologies in India points to this. The Vastness (literally, *Brahman*) cannot be bound by any laws, forms or concepts, however ingeniously devised. There can be sightings (*darshana*) of It, but It cannot be imprisoned in some exclusive formulation, as is attempted by the fundamentalists in all religions. The moment I think, "*This* alone is the Vastness," I reduce it to some smallness. One of the wonderful sayings of the Buddha: "It is not wise for a person to think 'This alone is Truth and none other.' "

Madame de Dampierre said, "One day a paper was found in which Gurdjieff was speaking of a 'law of nine'. Maybe it became later the 'law of seven'. He did not want people to become fixed and rigid, claiming 'This is this; this is what this means.' He always wanted us to be bewildered about what was said, so that we would turn to what we understand truly, what we know ourselves, to be able to go further from that."

One can see how ideas and practices become fixed once they are set down and partisans of this idea or that practice arise. The very ideas and practices which are intended to wake us up can become soporific. All the great teachers say in one way or another, and it is specifically said many times in the Gospels, "You have ears but you do not hear; you have eyes, but you do not see."

Madame de Dampierre said, "Once, in a Movements class, Gurdjieff needed six words. He thought of 'Father', 'Mother', 'Brother', 'Sister', 'Myself'. He asked for the sixth word. Someone suggested 'Idiot'. He laughed and took it. Now there are people who are reading deep and profound meaning in it, and in its placing. They take all this too seriously. He was often having fun."

One cannot help admiring those who search diligently for the meaning of special words—particularly in *Beelzebub*, which especially lends itself to such exertions. This must help them to stay close to the text. The mind needs to be occupied; otherwise it engages itself with the fluctuation of the price of cotton in Egypt, or some other thing. One cannot stay long inside the temple where the mysteries are played. One might as well stay in the general precincts and make measurements of the thickness of the walls of the temple, and engage in other such occupations which are necessary for the maintenance of the temple. There is always the risk that one may be excessively attracted by the merchandise sold around the temple, or be too taken by the interesting flora and fauna in the Port o' Monkeys as in René Daumal's *Mount Analogue*.

All traditions say that the mind has to be quieted so that something higher can be received. Perhaps informing the mind with the right ideas is a way of quieting it. Are not the ideas a part of the science of being which was brought by Gurdjieff? I remember Madame de Salzmann saying in New York many years ago, "Ideas, music and Movements in Gurdjieff's teaching supplement each other. One is not complete or whole without the other two."

On the other hand, she also said to me recently, "Now you don't need ideas. You need facts. What you know directly is a fact."

Talking about the great forms, such as the Chartres Cathedral or Indian mythology, Madame de Dampierre again raised the question of what effect it has on one directly. "Otherwise, one can select an idea or symbol from somewhere and say this is what it corresponds to in the Work. In that case, the Work ideas become limiting; they stop the action of these other great symbols and myths on me."

I saw this as important. One needs to be very careful while studying great traditions or great works of art so that one does not end up making an associative dictionary in which one claims that x in system A means y in system B.

Madame de Dampierre said, "If you had not seen Madame de Salzmann so often, I would have asked you, 'What question are you taking with you?' but now there is no need." Still, I found it a very good and necessary question. What is my inquiry now?

She said, "Madame de Salzmann was the one real disciple Gurdjieff had. Maybe all his work was directed only for her."

I was very struck by this remark. There can be many beneficiaries, students and pupils of a master, but to be a disciple is not easy, as one sees so clearly in the Gospels. The whole burden of the teaching, its very life, depends on the willingness of the disciples to sacrifice everything of their own and to be completely transformed by the teaching. I see in my case 'me, me, me' always asserts itself.

I was reminded of what Dr. Welch once said to me during a period of intensive work in Armonk, near New York, looking over the couple of hundred or so people gathered there: "Probably no more than one or two of these will be transformed. Maybe this whole thing is organized for one or two."

From the point of view of the ego, this is a chilling thought. But somewhere I understand that this has to be true: all the stones are needed to build a pyramid, not only the ones close to the apex.

I told Madame de Dampierre how moved I have been by some of the quiet Movements, more focused on inner sensation. "I have often felt a deep feeling, akin to remorse, but it is not only remorse. Something else is also there—a sense of connection with something immeasurably higher."

She said, "There are two categories of Movements and they proceed in opposite ways. In quiet Movements, one can be related with a higher world and one sees one's remoteness from it; and one has remorse. In these Movements, one has been freed from the usual worldly movements, and the music and the slow gestures all help one relate with the higher world, and one is quiet and receptive. The stronger Movements do the same by affirmation. I affirm myself, but only because I am related with a higher energy."

New York, 1971; Paris, June 1980.

To Relate the Higher
with the Lower

Madame de Salzmann suggested that I try to meditate sitting on a chair as well as cross-legged on the floor as I usually do. It is important not to get attached to only one particular posture in which one can work. Also, she repeated the necessity of working often, not for long at any one time, but frequently.

She has said several times, and in different ways, that Michel and I will understand each other. "You and Michel have something the same. He is very honest. I think you can work with him."

He has been very busy and I have not been able to spend much time with him so far. It was useful to go to Holland. I was very touched by the attention and hospitality of the people in the Work in Holland. Michel was especially generous. I was particularly affected by Josée de Salzmann's Movements class which consisted of slow, quiet work, trying to be open and available to a light in different parts of oneself. I had such a strong feeling, mostly of remorse, that at the end of the class I just stood there and wept.

When I was in Holland, Michel asked me to respond in his group of about fifty people. I saw how agitated and imitative I was, particularly in the first fifteen minutes or so. I could see clearly that I was not internally related. Later, perhaps because of the group energy, I was related to something quieter and more essential in myself. My head was much clearer; I could see myself and others more transparently and simply. I saw most of the group was as if asleep, as I myself had been earlier, and no doubt would soon be again. I saw clearly the need to work with other people. I realized the need to have a lot more people in our own group. I see it is necessary for my own sake. A way must be found.

Madame de Salzmann said that I was understanding much better than I did when I came, not only with the mind but also with the body. I hope she is right. She advised me, "Don't breathe forcefully. Paying attention to the breathing can help, but the important thing is the connection between the body and the head."

As my time in Paris came to a close, I was mindful of the extreme generosity of Madame de Salzmann in terms of time and attention. I asked her: "How can I say 'thank you'?"

"By working. We shall see. Maybe later you will be asked to do something which cannot be asked from others." She added, "Of course, come again. Come for longer if you wish. Next May is good, but I will let you know if there is some other time which is more suitable."

Madame de Salzmann asked me to describe to her the movement of energy inside the body. I told her that there is much more connection if the energy moves from the head, down the back, underneath the body and up the chest, rather than from the head down the chest. She said that the former is the right direction. The head needs to connect with the lower centers in the body before feeling emerges. It cannot go the other way. "At present this is sufficient. If you work on this at least once a day then we'll speak of the next step, maybe in America.

"Give my very good feeling to your wife. And to the Welches and Jessmin Howarth. I like very much Dr. Welch. He and I have been together through many things. I am very happy you came. Maybe we will meet soon in America."

Was it worthwhile to have come to Paris? Yes! First of all, purely negatively. I would have spent six weeks somewhere—Kyoto, New York, Halifax. Time passes in any case. The whole experience was a little like when I had initially come to Canada many years ago. Then as now, I had been lost in the outside world—largely because of my difficulty with the language—therefore I was thrown more on inner resources. But, much more importantly, I have learned something. I have a sense of the direction of the Work and how to work. I have no idea what will happen to the Work after the death of Madame de Salzmann. No doubt the same question was there towards the end of Gurdjieff's life.

Now I go back to my own life, my group, my habits. How can I put into practice and deepen what I have learned? If something real is understood, it will naturally be transmitted to others.

The Spirit needs a body; the work needs forms. There is formless freedom and there is incarnation. Everything is in the body. But, one cannot take the body personally. It is good to remember what Madame de Salzmann said, "Your body is not only yours. You need to work in order to relate the higher with the lower. That is the purpose of human existence."

Paris, May–June 1980; Holland, May 1980; Halifax, June 1980.

The Purpose of Human Existence

Without the relationship with higher energy, life has no meaning. The higher energy is the permanent Self, but you have no connection with that. For that connection, a fine substance needs to be generated. Otherwise, the energy of the body is too low to make contact with the very high energy which comes from above. You must persist—stay in front of the lack. Gradually, arrange to be in conditions which help you.

❖

A group of people is needed for a certain level of energy to appear. You must work alone and also with other people—often.

❖

There is an energy which is trying to evolve. That is why it comes into a body. If a person works and helps the evolution of this energy, at death this energy goes to a higher level. If one does not work, the energy returns to its own level. But the human life is wasted.

❖

The whole work is about energies. One must understand the relationship of energies, inside oneself and outside in the groups. There is an exchange possible. That is what the work is about. You must work often during the day, with others and by yourself.

❖

The relationship between the mind—the higher mind—and the body is the most direct thing to work on. When these two energies come together, then something new will be born.

More intensity and higher tempo are needed in the body, so that it will equal the mind in its force. Only then they can be related with each other.

❖

Ideas, music and Movements in Gurdjieff's teaching supplement each other. One is not complete or whole without the other two.

❖

Your body is not only yours. You need to work in order to relate the higher with the lower. That is the purpose of human existence.

There Are No Miracles

In spite of the difficulties, it was worthwhile to go to Paris and to spend six weeks there. Blessed by the overflowing generosity of Madame de Salzmann in terms of time, attention and energy, and also of other senior people in the Work, I had gradually begun to understand the direction of the Work and how to work. I had begun to realize that everything is in the body. I had been reading this for decades among the sayings of the Buddha, but I had not understood it earlier. I kept recalling what Madame de Salzmann had said: "Your body is not only yours. You need to work in order to relate the higher with the lower. That is the purpose and function of human existence."

As the summer moved on, the visits with Madame de Salzmann began to seem very far away, as if they had taken place a long time ago. I was no longer able to remember with any vividness what I had understood in her presence. What had been entirely clear and imperative then, now seemed like a good idea which would perhaps be useful to practice sometime.

I wrote to Madame de Salzmann describing my inner situation. She wrote back in September, 1980:

> I was interested by your letter. What you feel is quite normal—an insufficiency, a lack of intensity of perception, a lack of freedom in the ordinary mind—and—a feeling which is not there and which would give me the force to be in front of any condition.

I will be glad to see you again. I intend to come to New York just at the end of November for two months in any case. Come when it will suit you. But phone me in advance. I am preparing to work on the film of Movements which I intend to do—a hard work—but important. Movement is something difficult to understand.

I will be glad to speak with you about it.

When I met Madame de Salzmann in New York, she spoke about the Movements film which she was planning to make. I had some general questions about the Movements and some specific ones about an experiment I was trying. She asked me which Movements I was speaking about. I quickly showed her the beginning of the movement called "Forty Positions". Because I had merely taken the external positions of the movement without any inner attention, simply to show her which movement I was speaking about, she said, "That is not right. It is very important to do the Movements by containing and watching the movement of energy inside. Most Movements teachers don't understand this. When the arm is placed somewhere, the energy should go only that far, no further."

I realized how stupidly and mechanically I had taken the positions. I had not made a gesture which could be called 'sacred' in any sense. I said I had only showed the positions; but she was not satisfied. She was not interested in my explanations and excuses and asked me to try afresh. I showed her the positions again; this time with some inner attention. She seemed satisfied, and spoke about the Movements at length. I told her that sometimes I am more collected when walking or doing some other simple physical movements rather than while sitting quietly. She said, "That can be very useful. First sit quietly, then walk, then do simple movements which are not too complex. Vary the movements and the tempo; study what you find useful."

Then suddenly she said, "I have been thinking about you and I don't know what you are trying. How do you work?"

I told her and showed her what I could. She said, "That is right. Tomorrow maybe I shall give an exercise which will help."

She talked about 'love' and 'God'. She said, "What religions call God is the higher level, above the mind, but understood through a higher part of the mind. Man is made to create a link between two levels, to receive energy from a higher level in order to have an action on the level below—not a reaction. You are a bundle of energy for that: to receive from above and to act below. Unless you see it in practice, it remains mental. As long as the ego is dominant, nothing is possible."

Madame de Salzmann said that unless a sufficient number of people engage in conscious work, something undesirable is going to happen to humanity and to the planet. I had a feeling and some clarity that one needs to work for the sake of the whole Earth and the life on it; otherwise, all existence here would gradually get relegated to the outer darkness where there will be gnashing of teeth, as is said in the Bible. We may not be able to work for the cosmos as a whole—that is too far removed from our level—but we can work for the Earth.

❖ ❖ ❖

In the group meeting later, Madame de Salzmann repeated, even in the same words, what she had said to me earlier in our meeting. "Man is made to create a link between two levels—to receive energy from a higher level in order to have an action on the level below; not a reaction." What keeps amazing me is that I sometimes see this so clearly, without any doubt or confusion, but then, very soon, I behave as if I have never heard it. The next time, when she repeats it, or I should say when she demonstrates it again, it strikes me anew.

Transformation is the result of seeing. Madame de Salzmann speaks about it again and again. I am just beginning to understand why the Gospels report so many miracles. Only an extraordinary event or presence can take us out of our ordinary mind. But, we fall back again and again. Miracles are all internal. When the disciples' level is transformed, even fleetingly, from water into wine, they say, "Lord, we believe," which means, "We see." However, before long one forgets and no longer sees. Very soon after a great miracle the disciples carry on as if nothing had been understood. Only in the presence of teachers does there seem to be light and clarity. Away from them, darkness and confusion prevail. In their presence even ordinary water tastes like wine. Left to oneself, even one's wine soon loses its taste. The transformation of perceptions is miraculous; and this miracle needs to be repeated again and again.

In my next meeting with Madame de Salzmann, during one of the relatively lighter moments we often had after working intensely for half an hour or so, I said to her that I was going to refer to her as Our Lady of Perpetual Miracle! She smiled, and was quiet for a few moments. Then she said, "There are no miracles. It is all a play of forces. You can read it in your own sacred books."

Then she spoke about Sri Anirvan, who apparently had said something similar. She was very interested in hearing about my meeting with Sri Anirvan a few years earlier. He had been ill, and was to die soon after, and lay in bed during our meeting. Among the things he had said, I had been most struck by his last remark to me: "You would know something true when you realize that 'God' is the same as 'dog'". She listened intently, was quiet for a few moments, and said, "The same, but also different."

❖ ❖ ❖

In a group meeting I asked about the fear of transformation. Something in me does not really wish to be transformed. Something in me did not even really want to ask this question. In that sense what I asked was insincere. I forced myself to ask this question even though I realized that it was not really a serious or a burning question for me. I did not wish to give in to the inner passivity I was feeling, and I knew from past experience that by asking a question I invited her gaze to fall on me. If she engaged with my question, then it was difficult for me to remain wholly passive. Madame de Salzmann spoke about the perfectly lawful resistance and passivity. She said, "One needs to find a more active attention that can overcome the passivity. Then a real inner action will take place; and thus a transformation."

❖ ❖ ❖

In a meeting with Madame de Salzmann this afternoon I understood something rather important: I understood that the sensation of the body and the sense of the presence of I in the body are different. While engaged with the usual activities it is necessary to maintain a sense of one's general presence. Sometimes, as an aid to that awareness of presence, it is useful to sense one particular limb or another.

The energy of the body is not the same thing as a sensation of the body. Sensation is a way to relate the energy of the body with the energy of the mind. Even theoretically, except at the very highest level, no energy can exist by itself, alone. As Madame de Salzmann put it, "There is no loneliness. Everything is in relation with other levels. If the energy of the body is not related to something higher, it will be taken by something lower.

"Energy of the higher mind is required, from above the head, outside the body. This has to come together with the energy of the body. It takes time. Being without tension helps. The mind has to be very deeply quiet.

"Do you see the separation of the head and the body? If you feel deeply the sense of the lack of this connection, then you begin to need it and to work for it.

"When one gives attention inside, then the two energies, rather than going their own ways and at their own rates, are oriented towards each other. Then they move towards each other. Then feeling arises. They may not come together, but already there is a difference inside. It is very fragile; any movement can break it. So one tries to practice moving slowly, walking, listening or speaking.

"Impressions are the most important thing. It is not easy to receive impressions without reacting.

"In order to be related with a higher level, some freedom is necessary from the level of existence where one is. Passivity of the body and of the mind stands in the way. The process requires active attention."

I said that I recognize the bondage created by self-importance. Self-importance is what keeps me tied to the ordinary level, and that is what robs me of the freedom to be related with something higher. I asked, "Why do I want to be special? I see that so much energy is wasted in that."

She said, "The important thing is to be. If there is no real I, then the ego takes over. Energy cannot be without relationship. If it does not serve I intentionally, then it automatically serves the ego."

A line from a Chinese classic flashed through my mind. I had seen it several years ago quoted in a letter written by Mao Tse Tung to his wife. It said, "When the lion is departed from the mountain, the monkey becomes the king." In what must have been a moment of clear sight, Mao Tse Tung had added, "And I have become the king." I saw that we create a Port o' Monkeys everywhere, even on the mountain slope, simply because in us, the monkey is the king.

Madame de Salzmann looked at me and smiled. She said, "A few days is a very short time. Come for longer. You may come in May or June to Paris; it does not matter when."

As I left, I pondered the remarks Madame de Salzmann had made just before my mind wandered off to China: "The important thing is to be. If there is no real I, then the ego takes over. Energy cannot be without relationship. If it does not serve I intentionally, then it automatically serves the ego."

Paris, June 1980; New York, December 1980.

The Work Is Not Done
by the Ego

At a group meeting in New York last evening, in answer to some-one's question about the fear of death, Madame de Salzmann said, "Energies of different qualities have different durations. The energy of a higher level does not die at the death of a lower level. At the death of the body, not all the energies in the body die. These higher energies are in the body, but they are not of the body.

"The work is not only sensing one's right arm. Why all this sensing? Our attention is so scattered that it needs to be trained to be contained in the body, to relate with it, to remain anchored. These exercises are necessary; but that is not the work. The basic idea of the work is that our centers are not in harmony. But why should you believe this? Do you see this? Do you see what you lose when you are in pieces? The work is to bring these centers in harmony, so that there will be higher intelligence.

"When you see active attention losing itself in passivity, it is important not to try to do something, but to stay in front of it and to suffer it. That seeing is what produces new knowledge. You don't suffer enough."

Later on, at the Welches' apartment, there was a reading from the notes of Gurdjieff's Paris group. The reading was much to the point and very practical. It spoke about the need of struggling with oneself, in practice, not only in theory. It advised the pupils to take a definite time and decide to work at that time. If one cannot work, one should read about it, think about it or talk about it. Even if one does nothing related with the work, one should not do anything else; just stay. Link it with a strong habit, such as cigarette smoking or eating. Do not smoke if you do not carry out what you have decided.

I did not want to be carried away by enthusiasm, but I felt strongly that I needed to struggle with myself in practice, in day-to-day life, otherwise, I have only theories and fine words. I realized I need a practice of inner work. Whatever I think of doing, I find myself already making excuses. What is needed is a continual renewal of the practice of work.

It is no use pitying myself, or lamenting my lack of understanding or will. When Madame de Salzmann advises, "If necessary, punish the body," I refuse to hear it. Suddenly, I do not understand it or I refuse to accept it. Then I turn around, in a few days or weeks, and ask for help. I bemoan the fact that nobody is telling me directly what I need to do, that there is no intensity. I ought to be ashamed of myself. What could be more direct advice than, "If necessary, punish the body"? Ah, the self-justifications and deceptions that one goes through!

❖ ❖ ❖

It was Valentine's Day, so I decided to take some flowers to Madame de Salzmann. The maid wanted to take the flowers I had brought, as was her custom. I said I would like to give the flowers to Madame myself. The maid, a large black woman, was sweet and said, "Be a lover boy!" I gave the flowers to Madame de Salzmann, and with them a Valentine's Day kiss. She looked pleased and said emphatically, "*Merci, monsieur.*"

But only a few moments were allowed for these personal pleasantries. Madame de Salzmann called me to work. She so much emphasized the need for having an action on the ordinary level of life. "This teaching is not to make us angels, but to make us men."

We drove to the Foundation where Lord Pentland had arranged for Madame de Salzmann to see a videotape of a talk by Fritjof Capra and myself which the San Francisco group had organized the previous year. It was interesting to see the videotape in the company of Madame de Salzmann. Her presence changed my perceptions, and I could see myself on the video a little more impartially than otherwise. I was slower in my talking than I had realized, and a lot more tense, even aggressive.

❖ ❖ ❖

I asked Madame de Salzmann, "How can I be sure that I am experiencing precisely what you are speaking about? It is possible simply to imagine that I understand you. I wish to be clear about the connection between the energy of the body and the energy of the mind." I asked her to watch me while I tried inwardly to come to this connection. She was very attentive and acute about my internal states. Occasionally she would remark that at this moment I had the right connection or at that, I had lost it.

Now I have a better idea what this connection between the energy of the body and of the mind is. It is not a specific sensation of a particular limb but a generalized sense of presence in the body. A particular sensation can help in this, but if it is too strong, it can even detract. She said not to force attention, or the union of energies, but to watch. That, by itself, will bring about the union, to a greater or a lesser degree, but she emphasized again that there is no need either to brutalize the body or the mind, or to ignore them. "This work is not done by the ego. The ego is not the body or the mind."

I see clearly that without a relationship between the body and the mind, my life has little significance. A new energy, or force, does arise when this relationship is made, but it is certainly not the case that I have any control over this connection. I see that the higher cannot be conquered; it needs to be wooed, with attention and care.

I recounted my meeting with Madame de Salzmann to Dr. and Mrs. Welch. They were both very interested in what I had asked Madame de Salzmann, namely, to watch and to comment as I tried to pay attention internally to uniting the energy of the mind with that of the body. Dr. Welch remarked that it was like asking her to give me biofeedback information about my internal states.

Later on, my mind wondered if Madame de Salzmann could actually see my internal states. Are one's internal states really visible to sensitive eyes? That is certainly my impression of her.

❖ ❖ ❖

When I next went to Paris I was met at the airport by a friend who took me directly to the Maison, where a day of work was in progress. We arrived just in time for lunch. Madame de Salzmann spoke about the necessity of working intentionally, not only for oneself, but for the world. "The world needs certain vibrations which are produced only when some people work intentionally."

When I met with Madame de Salzmann after lunch. She was, as always, generous and direct. She said that I could go to all the meetings and classes I was in last year, plus a group of hers on Wednesdays. She said again that I should get to know Michel. "He has something special. He was brought up by Mr. Gurdjieff until the age of twenty or so. Mr. Gurdjieff planted something essential in him."

I told her that I did not want to be a pest, nor did I want to waste my time. I was here basically to receive her vibrations, and asked her if she had any time. "Yes, I shall find time. Maybe not tomorrow because I was not expecting you. After that I can arrange things. Also, I shall go to London for ten days on the twenty-fifth of May. You can come with me, if you wish. Wait and see."

❖ ❖ ❖

Madame de Salzmann said, "You must tell me how you work with your group."

I was just thinking about what to say when she asked me what I wanted. I said, "I want to taste, in fact, to eat, knowledge. I have read many things; I can give lectures on them, but I don't know directly. I wish to know directly."

She said, "*Par la sensation ... une sensation suffisante.*"

It felt right. I wish for that sensation which would be really sufficient, a sensation which can be touched, which can be cut. She said, "For that, attention is needed. An attention which is much faster. Ideas are necessary, but they are not sufficient. Direct knowledge is needed.

"One needs to see that one is in pieces. Stay in front of that, and suffer for it. Then, a new feeling arises which can change something. The work is not turning the mind to the body. The ordinary mind must be absolutely quiet; only then can the higher mind be related with the body. This requires attention, active attention."

I said I make excuses for myself. She said, "It is not I, but self-love that makes excuses."

I wondered what would assist the cultivation of this active, direct attention. She said, "Seeing that I am in pieces and that I need unity."

Halifax, February 1981; New York, February 1981; Paris, May 1981.

Intensity Is Needed

It is necessary to guard against the enchantment of activities and busy-ness and against the entrapment of self-importance. It is difficult to remain internally quiet and to refrain from doing something or other. I see that I wish to be busy with a lot of activities, especially those which give me the appearance of being important. I need to see that I am not important. I am an ordinary man, a man who sometimes wishes to know himself, but who cannot truly know himself as long as he remains the way he is.

I need to remember that I am not here in Paris for anything other than to learn what Madame de Salzmann can teach me. I need to wait and be in attendance. It would be foolish of me to be out seeing Paris or attending French lessons when she calls. I do not know when she might call, therefore I need to be always available. Otherwise, I would waste my time. I need to remember why I have come, not only to Paris right now, but also why I have come into this body and into this world.

I met with Madame de Salzmann this evening for nearly an hour and a half. She is absolutely amazing! Each time I see her she asks me how I work. She pins me down: "How do you work? How do you have sensation? What means attention? Right now, if you work, what do you do?"

What is required? To quiet the mind completely, to have no tensions. To fight the mind does not help. One needs to see that one is not related; then one is interested in the relationship. She said, "Religions talk about it as 'self-surrender'. But they mean it in a different way because they have lost the central idea.

"Intensity is needed. Work at least three or four times a day, for twenty minutes to half an hour. When one opens one's eyes, one sees differently. But there is a moment when a sort of explosion takes place inside. It is difficult to explain it. But only then transformation is possible. Work on it for two or three days, then speak to me. Try to keep some inner attention when meeting other people, or doing anything else. Intensity, more intensity. Otherwise, one wastes time."

She said, "You should get to know Michel. Also Pauline de Dampierre. She has a good way to bring younger people to sensation inside. Perhaps they can come to your place when they visit New York." Emboldened, I wondered if she herself could come. She considered it for a few moments, smiled, and said, "I am very busy with the film. But you must meet Michel.... I shall phone you tomorrow. Perhaps you can come and have lunch with us tomorrow."

She said she would let me read some notes of Mr. Gurdjieff's lectures and questions-answers, and asked me not to copy them. I was again reminded of the burden of responsibility she carries and how she has to watch for every pupil's situation and needs.

❖ ❖ ❖

It is incredible that with all the time on my hands I still managed to be five minutes late for my appointment with Madame de Salzmann. I went in feeling a certain remorse of conscience for my tardiness.

Madame de Salzmann seemed to be in an unusually warm mood. Again she expressed her wish that I would make contact with Michel. In the middle of our conversation, apropos of nothing that I could see, she said it would be nice if Michel could join us. "I shall go see if he is there." So she went and knocked on his door. Poor Michel. This was hardly what he needed. He had a cold; he is always very busy and there are so many people who want his time. Nevertheless, he came and we spoke together a little. She left us alone, as if arranging a discreet rendezvous between shy lovers. We arranged to have lunch together in a few days. He said he might even come and give a 'workshop' in Halifax.

❖ ❖ ❖

I told Madame de Salzmann that when I listen to her in English, there is a different impact than when she speaks in French. It seems more profound in French. I was thinking particularly of the group meeting the previous evening. She said that last evening she was very direct because the group is ready for it.

I reported to her that the previous evening, during the meditation sitting, I was able to go deep inside myself. There was a different vibration, another sort of breathing, and another quality of presence, even though I was often unconnected with what the person leading the meditation was saying. As soon as I mentioned the name of the person, she immediately offered to introduce me to him. "You can work with him. Call him, speak to him. Tell him that I sent you."

I was touched by her generosity. "Anyone you wish to see or work with, it can be arranged."

I told her about a recurring feeling I have had, particularly during the last year, that the question is not what the cosmos or the Work can do for me, but what can I do for them. Not what they are for me, but what am I for them? Also, I told her about the feeling I had had, particularly after a recent meditation sitting, of the complete triviality of my occupations and mental machinations. I live as if the whole cosmos was designed for my benefit, and for me to get ahead. She was interested in what I had to say and said it was all true. "This is why one needs to work. To have a different relation with the world. Human beings are links between two levels. One needs to learn to work consciously in order to pay for one's existence."

I asked her for the readings based on the notes of Gurdjieff's talks which she had mentioned previously. She went in and got four, all in English. I wondered if I could have some in French also. She went in again to fetch some. I congratulated myself a little for my cleverness, for this way I would get more readings, some in English and some in French. She brought a reading in French, but demanded an English reading back in exchange. It was clear that she would give me a total of four readings only. I could have them in French if that is what I wished. Too bad, I thought to myself, I would have certainly benefited more from a reading in English. I should not have tried to be so clever and should have relied upon her discernment.

She said, "Come on Sunday at eleven. Be exact, for the door is closed. You read these by then. We can talk about them."

❖ ❖ ❖

Madame de Salzmann advised against giving up ordinary life completely at present. "Sometimes, one would like to. But what would one do if one were not engaged with this level? When I was young, I liked to go to restaurants, go dancing, and do other things. When I listened to people like Krishnamurti, I was very impressed. But I did not want to give up dancing. I wanted to be like them, but not all the time. Gradually, with Mr. Gurdjieff, I found out what is more interesting than going dancing, and that one could live like that all the time. Unless one is interested in something else, something higher, one cannot and need not give up the level of activity one is in. The body also needs something. One needs to work at the level where one is. You cannot change the level unless something higher holds your attention."

She said, "In the beginning, for a long time, one reads, discusses ideas, practices Movements, works with other people, and many other such things. Then comes a time when that is not enough. One needs to understand directly what it means that the centers are not connected. Ideas cannot give the necessary energy. The higher part of the mind needs to be connected with the body."

We worked together, and she asked, as she has often done in the past, if this is what I needed. "Do you see that you need this relationship? It can come about only if one stays in front of one's inadequacy and suffers for it. One cannot do it, but still one is responsible for it."

Paris, May 1981.

Body and Mind Are Not Related

I had a meeting with Madame de Dampierre yesterday. For her, pondering something means trying to stay in front of it. Gradually the question broadens, many relations emerge, but still the question is enclosed by the unknown. She had read a book by Stella Kramerisch on Hindu art, and wondered if the Indian temples and sculptures speak of the flow of energies as the Work does, for as she said, "The flow of energies is the central thing in the Work."

We spoke of Madame de Salzmann, and I said, "She is marvelous." Also, I said that Madame de Salzmann is a one-note musician. Having found the right and true note, she plays only that, calling attention again and again to the one thing needful. Madame de Salzmann is interested in the central practice of "bringing the energy of the mind in contact with the energy of the body."

Madame de Dampierre was not quite satisfied with what I had said. She said, "Madame de Salzmann is not merely marvelous. She is more than that. Besides, she does not always say the same thing; there is always a subtle difference."

❖ ❖ ❖

There was a reading at the Maison of a lecture Gurdjieff had given in New York in the forties. I found it very interesting. Among other things, it said, when a child is four to five years old, it is the time to begin teaching about sex. You have your own experience to help you.

Very rarely are children trained normally on this side, and we only find out what is wrong when the damage is done. Seventy-five per cent of thought and feeling comes from sex. It manifests itself night and day and everything is colored by it. In Asia sex education is a part of religious rites, and the results are excellent.

We have a moon inside us, as well as a sun, and other things. We are a whole system. If you know what your moon is and what it does you can understand the cosmos.

The idea of a human being able to internally mirror the external cosmos occurs in so many traditions. There surely must be levels in us analogous to the level of the moon and that of the sun. I spent a long time pondering about what my moon is.

❖ ❖ ❖

In a meeting with Madame de Salzmann, she asked me, as she has many times, "What do you try with your groups?" I told her about the various activities we undertake: the study of ideas, the exchange of observations, Movements, repairs and maintenance in the Work House on Sundays, crafts and quiet work. She said that one could engage in crafts, ideas and everything else and not be in the Work. We spoke a little about the bewitchment of the crafts—in fact of all kinds of doing—and about the fragility of real work.

She is always trying to draw attention to another dimension or another level on which a connection with real work exists, and from which we are continually distracted by one activity or another. I said we seem everywhere to create a Port o' Monkeys. We are fascinated by the flora and fauna we find, forgetting the mountain which we had at some stage wished to climb. I said that I can get lost in the study of special words in *Beelzebub*, or in the study of symbolism in the Gospels, and other such studies in the groups. "Surely," I said, "these studies are only tools." She agreed.

I told her about working with others in quiet work. I myself am more related then. "Of course," she said. I told her how I sometimes feel as if my role is to be like a good metal conductor that conducts electricity from one level to another. But often I want to possess this energy and use it, rather than letting it use me. She was very interested, and said, "How to let this energy, which is there, act on me—on my mind and body—so that a transformation can take place?"

We talked about many things. She had been interested in my reference to *Mount Analogue*, and told me that she had brought René Daumal to Mr. Gurdjieff.

I told her, "For a long time I have had a feeling that the only thing which will give any sense to my life is to be of use to some higher purpose than myself."

She said, "Right now, the most necessary thing is to see, in fact, that your body and mind are not related, and to stay in front of that and to suffer for your inadequacy. Work often, but not for long, because it takes much energy; and sense the difference in levels between when you are related and when you are ordinary."

❖ ❖ ❖

Sometimes I have a strong desire to escape from my ordinary life—with all its resentments, aggravations and waste of energy. Then I have a wish to avoid having anything to do with the world, my job, my family or the neighbors. But I see that inaction is not the way to freedom from the entanglements of action. In any case, I cannot escape from the superficial by avoiding an engagement with 'ordinary' life because I carry my usual and trivial self wherever I go.

Can one really avoid all aggravation and difficulty in life? Or does one need to learn how to be related with something higher in the midst of difficulty? In any case, as Krishna says, one does not avoid the bondage of action by inaction. Only by learning what will make action sacred can I be free of resentment and anxiety. There is an intimate spiral of knowing, doing and being—three threads woven together. One of these cannot make sense apart from the other two. If I were really wise, that is, if I really saw what is good for my soul, I should be sending

flowers to those who make my life so difficult, for they can be internally useful. That does not mean, of course, that one needs to get sentimental, and agree to whatever they want. In the *Mahabharata* battle,
Duryodhana was necessary for the evolution of Arjuna, yet that did not
mean Duryodhana could be allowed to continue his selfish acts.

The world is necessary; resistance is necessary. All religions want
people to fly to Heaven, and they behave as if the world is a mistake.
Religion believes that ordinary life is illusory; science thinks that
Heaven is not real. We who feel that we are children of both Heaven
and Earth cannot be partial. The so-called 'fall' of humanity is necessary. The expulsion of Adam and Eve from the Garden of Eden is also
a sending forth. Having understood something, Adam and Eve are sent
out to test themselves in the world. In the film, *Meetings with Remarkable
Men*, the seeker is sent back into the world in order to test his understanding of the real meaning of inner struggle.

I had been musing on this theme practically all day. When I came
to see Madame de Salzmann in the evening, the first thing she said was,
"It is necessary to develop the ability to have an action on the ordinary
level." She emphasized this with great force. The remark that she had
made to me a few months ago, that this teaching is not given in order
to make us angels, but to make us truly human, seemed unusually clear
to me now.

❖ ❖ ❖

As I entered Madame de Salzmann's room at the Maison for the meeting
at seven o'clock, she said that it was not my meeting and that I was
supposed to come at eight. I was sure that she was mistaken. The women
met at eight and in any case I had been there last week at seven. I had
no doubt that I was supposed to be there. So she said, "Okay, come in!"
As I came into the small room, it was clear that something had been
changed in the schedule. This was a meeting of four or five of the most
senior people in the Work and it certainly was not my meeting. But

there I was; having made such strong protestations, I could hardly leave. So I stayed.

Although my body was not quite connected, I kept trying. Madame de Salzmann was very forceful. Speaking about the energy from a higher level, she said something which I had always felt to be true, but she gave it such a direct—almost a physical—meaning. She said, "Religious people talk about the Lord, *Seigneur*. That is an energy of a very high level. They say, 'The Lord helps me.' That is true. But something is required of me. I have to prepare myself for this *Seigneur* to help."

Afterwards, Mr. William Segal, who had been at the meeting, spoke to me, commenting on the force and clarity with which I had spoken and the way I had held my ground. He said, "It was a real Zen moment. I would like to take you out to dinner for that." Over dinner he asked me what I made of Madame de Salzmann's statement that the health of the Earth depended on some people working consciously. "Do you think that your work affects the Earth?"

I told him that I could not say that I know this, but this idea makes a great deal of sense to me. It is surely a way of saying that there is a larger purpose to my existence than ego satisfaction. Besides, I grew up in India where the notion that the Earth is alive is still strong. One of the Upanishads says, "The Earth meditates." Modern science has de-spiritualised our view of the planets and of the Sun. However, even in contemporary celebrations of science, it is possible to find the notion that human beings are the mind of the Earth, if not of the whole cosmos.

I told him that I find it engaging to ponder and live with the idea which I have often heard from Madame de Salzmann: "Man can serve the Earth by becoming a link between two levels. He can receive energy from a higher level in order to have an action on the level below; not a reaction."

Paris, May 1981.

Unless One Prepares Others

I found the day of work at the Maison very useful. It raised a question for me about what I am doing here. Why am I here? Why am I occupying a place here? What do I try inside? I see that I can soon convince myself that I did not really understand the task that was given, or that it was too abstract or that it was not really helpful. There are at least three things one can always try: one, to economize on expenditure of energy. Therefore, one can try to reduce physical tensions and negative emotions and turning thoughts. Also, to use only the right amount of energy while doing a job, that is, whatever part of the body is used, force should be concentrated only there. The rest of the body should be relaxed. Two, to be a little mindful of one's breathing. Three, to sense one part or another in the body and to come to the state when I can utter, "I am." It is like a prayer which slowly helps deepen sensation, especially if I do not give explanations as to why this is not useful.

If one does not utilize the time to work consciously when one is engaged in the forms of the Work, it is unlikely that one will attain something anywhere else.

I was not feeling well. Then I remembered something I was told Madame de Salzmann had said, as reported to me by a friend in Paris, that one should not be afraid of ailments. She had said that by being afraid, one produces wrong vibrations and creates problems. Fears and tensions associated with ailments create more problems than the ailments themselves. I am sure that most of the time I treat myself too preciously and tenderly. The body runs me rather than serving me. How can it serve anything higher than myself if it does not serve anything worthwhile even in me?

❖ ❖ ❖

When I saw Madame de Salzmann at the Maison, she was very busy and in a hurry. I hesitated for a little while but decided to try to meet her anyway. I recalled that on one occasion the previous year when I had had similar considerations—such as 'She is very busy,' 'I should not bother her,' or 'I don't have anything really important to raise, in any case, nothing which cannot wait'—I had decided not to telephone her and ask for a meeting. The next time we met she demanded to know why I had not called. I explained my reasoning, feeling no doubt a little virtuous about how I had considered her rightly. She had listened patiently looking at me intently and had said, "I have the freedom to say 'no'. You must call!"

As far as I was concerned, I was placed under the bonds of her care, and from that moment I was not free not to ask her. She could say "no" or "not now." It was her decision to see me or not to, not mine. Soon I began to realize how difficult it was for me actually to allow her the freedom to say "no." Something in me often felt as if I knew better what was good for me. On the occasions when she did say "no" or "later," I found myself taking it personally, as if it was a judgment on me. I see that I sense the need for help, and I seek out the right physician; then I insist on dictating the prescription to the doctor. Any help I receive seems to be in spite of myself.

In any case, I asked to see her now, even when it was obvious that she was extremely busy. She was very generous to me, and when I said that I did not wish to bother her because I knew she was busy, she practically growled at me, "Yes, I am busy. But I see who I wish to see."

Then we sat and talked and worked in her office. I described to her an unusual experience I had had in the meditation sitting the previous evening, and told her that this was the reason why I had wanted to see her. She had led the meditation and had given a forceful exercise.

Somewhat uncharacteristically, she had used strongly religious vocabulary during the meditation, and had spoken about the energy which brings about a new birth. Towards the end of the meditation I had experienced a sudden disappearance of all the tensions, or pressures, in the head. I could see my thoughts, which were very slowed down, and I watched them without much interest, as if they belonged to someone else. I walked home with a very light head, interested in understanding the state I was in: very slow thoughts, unusually clear head, clear vision, extraordinarily vibrant and bright colors. This state lasted about twenty minutes. Gradually, with the stimulation of advertisements in the street, traffic noises and a general air of agitation all around, the usual turning of thought returned, with the attendant tensions in the head. It was such a clear taste of another state.

Madame de Salzmann was interested in my description and asked for details. Then she said, "That is quite normal. It was worth coming to Paris just for that experience."

She seemed to be in no hurry to let me go. Several people were waiting outside in order to meet with her. I was feeling, or perhaps imagining, their negativity towards me, and also feeling a certain ego-satisfaction. But whenever I made a small movement to get up, she would ask me something else. It seemed as if she had all the time in the world and had nothing else to do but to chat with me. She was asking me questions such as whether my wife is in the Work, how many children I have and so on. I was now beginning to feel myself in a hurry, for I had a Movements class which had already begun ten minutes ago.

Madame de Salzmann had earlier told me that she would be going to London the next day and had asked me to come with her. Finally, she said, "Call me as soon as you get to London. Then I will tell you when I can see you. Maybe you come and have lunch with me in London the day after tomorrow. You should rest now. You need it."

❖ ❖ ❖

I see that I do not see the terror of my situation. I do not often see that I am nothing. I can talk of large ideas and I have ambitions. I have a store of ideas, associations and habits, and in each circumstance some combination of these represents me. I carry on with my dreams of glory, or of horror, occupied with my satisfactions and my resentments. I talk of sacrifice, I can hold forth on its place in religion, or in life, but in fact I do not sacrifice much. I do not want to give up anything, imagining that I really do own something. How true are the lines of René Daumal, in the notes at the end of his *Mount Analogue*:

> I am dead because I lack desire;
> I lack desire because I think I possess;
> I think I possess because I do not try to give.
> In trying to give, you see that you have nothing;
> Seeing you have nothing, you try to give of yourself;
> Trying to give of yourself, you see that you are nothing;
> Seeing you are nothing, you desire to become;
> In desiring to become, you begin to live.

The fact is that what I call myself, or my life, is a little pulse in the vast continuum of space-time-energy. There are billions of other pulses, some very large and some very small, and others in between, in this Vastness. By happenstance, I am related in different ways with a few other pulses. Like others, I shall disappear, and perhaps reappear elsewhere in another form. I have no idea whether there is a continuity or a direction in this movement of the pulse.

What am I called to do, in my own little corner of space-time? How do I listen? How do I respond? Apart from engaging with this question there is no meaning to my life.

In a meditation sitting in London, at an occasion which seemed to be a memorial service for Madame Lannes who had been in charge of the Work in England for many years, Madame de Salzmann said some very interesting things which I had not heard before. She said, "Unless one prepares others to take one's place and to occupy one's level, so that the right kind of vibration or energy is produced, one is not free to continue one's work in higher spheres. The best way to express our gratitude to our teachers is to work so that they do not have to come back to lower levels. If they are freed from the Earth, they can continue their work at higher levels. Otherwise, they are obliged to return and keep working here."

I was very struck by what she said. It seemed as if a given level of energy and functioning has to be maintained. It cannot be left vacant; the form cannot be left unfilled. The lower forms or levels will engage and hold me if they are not occupied by others. This is why, not only do the students need the teacher, but also the teacher needs the students. Otherwise, the teacher cannot be free of the present level of existence.

Paris and London, May 1981.

Ideas Alone Cannot
Change a Person

When I met with Madame de Salzmann in London, she began as if from zero; but gradually as she worked and as I worked she spoke more and more intensely. She said, "It is important to work often, to keep a sensation, to let the energy of the mind unite with the energy of the body. Ideas alone cannot change a person. Real transformation is brought by the higher energy—from above the head—coming into the body and acting on it. There is resistance, completely lawfully. Gradually, the body will recognize that this transformation is good for him too. Then he will cooperate. He should be given what he needs, not necessarily what he wants."

I told Madame de Salzmann about the feeling of a call from a deeper or a higher part of myself. I said that I did not have a very strong link with it. I told her about the experience the other day of feeling like one among billions of waves in the vast ocean of energy–space–time. She was very interested. I also told her about a dream I had had of Krishna shooting me with a revolver, rather than throwing his traditional discus. She wondered if my mind, which understands, is trying to goad the body into working.

❖ ❖ ❖

I see at least one of the functions that mechanical anxiety plays. It is a support of the ego. It seems that I need a certain level of anxiety to maintain a sense of 'me-ness', as if, 'I worry, therefore I am.' And almost anything will do. Worry and anxiety wrap themselves around anything. What they reveal is not the reality of anything, but the level of my consciousness. I go over the same things, again and again. Most of the time it is not necessary and it is a total waste of energy. But it is as if I shall not exist if this worrying does not give meaning to my life. A hurt or an anxiety, endlessly repeated, buttresses my sense of myself. It gives me security. I see that unless I bring attention, my energy is taken by this or that passing anxiety.

Isn't this what Madame de Salzmann has been saying? Energy at any level exists only in relation to an energy of another level. If my ordinary life energy is not channelled or used, it will be squandered. As she said, "Positive action is needed all the time. Constant vigilance." The ego resists being employed in the service of something higher; so it goes over this or that, maintaining its importance, worrying about its accounts: past hurts, pleasant memories and future pleasures. I need to ask, "What function does my energy serve?" In other words, "What do I serve?"

❖ ❖ ❖

Dr. and Mrs. Welch were also in London in connection with a memorial service for Madame Lannes. Mrs. Welch very much wanted to visit the grave of A.R. Orage, her first teacher in the Work. We went searching for it, and after some confusion we finally located the grave in the cemetery of Old Hampstead Church. On the gravestone, engraved by Eric Gill, is an enneagram and one of Orage's favorite verses from the *Bhagavad Gita*:

> The wise grieve neither for the living nor the dead
> Never at any time was I not, nor thou,
> Nor these princes of men, nor shall we ever cease to be.
> The unreal has no being.
> The real never ceases to be.

It was good to be able to recite a few of these verses for Mrs. Welch in Sanskrit. The *Bhagavad Gita* is invariably profound and challenging. I believe it is the single most important work to originate from India.

❖ ❖ ❖

I had a wonderful meeting with Madame de Salzmann in her London apartment. We worked for a while, then, as usual, we had a few minutes of general conversation. She was in no hurry to let me go and we talked about this and that. I told her that I had gone to see Krishnamurti the previous day. I had learned from an acquaintance that he was staying in Brockwood Park, not very far from London, for a few days and I had gone there to meet him. I said to her, "Krishnamurti always speaks about something beyond thought and time. And I always ask him how to reach this level of insight in time and by thought. We both seem to be helpless. I am here, he is there. We see each other at a distance and call to each other, but we cannot touch each other. There is not a real meeting. He inspires and he invites argument and discussion. But can any real transformation take place by discussion? Unless I can be helped to see how I might move from where I am stuck, he cannot be a guide for me."

Madame de Salzmann had much sympathy with what I said. I see that she is a guide for me because she sees my difficulty and reveals the requirement of positive action.

Later in the conversation when I was complaining about someone, she made a comment which stopped me and has since then become for me, in spite of its unusual grammatical construction, a very useful aphorism. She said, "It cannot not be the case that nobody is without no use."

Whenever I think of this remark, I cannot help smiling, and I realize again how a person who is free from the level of like and dislike can find every situation and every person of some value and use.

Madame de Salzmann talked about the exuberance of life. I said to her that one of the remarks of Ouspensky which has always struck me as rather odd is that laughter is a waste of energy and that Jesus Christ never laughed. I said that Ouspensky must have been a religious ascetic in spite of his protestations to the contrary. The Indian sages speak of *ananda* (delight) as a characteristic of the highest level. Surely, laughter is a form of *ananda*. How can Ouspensky say Christ never laughed? Madame de Salzmann laughed heartily.

After a while, she talked about the necessity of engagement with life. She said, "All the great teachers come back to the world, even though they understood something very high in a monastery or under a tree."

She was very interested in what Rajneesh had said about yoga in a book she had read. He said that all the religions forget that yoga is the only important thing. By 'yoga' he means a spiritual method of integration. Suddenly, I felt as if she was thinking about something and looking at me. Perhaps she was thinking how I might be useful. She asked if I did yoga and I told her the two classical postures I practiced daily. She asked many questions about my life, what I teach, and the like. She wanted me to spend more time in France, learn the language, come in the summers. She said that Michel had told her that he had asked me to speak on the *Bhagavad Gita* at the Maison in Paris and that she would come to hear me. While I wish her to come, I also fear her coming. Who in me wants to show off, and what is afraid? What is, is; one cannot pretend or hide.

❖ ❖ ❖

Madame de Salzmann reconfirmed the exercise in quiet work about which I had some questions, and warned me not to undertake it except with advanced pupils. Then she said, "You must work with others, even if there are only four or five. Then you understand more. Help them in quiet work. Must tell your wife what you learn."

She emphasized the Movements and how useful they are. She would like to show me some work in Movements in connection with the film; but not yet. The classes are not ready yet.

She suggested two exercises for me and said, "Write to me after three or four weeks, telling me what these exercises have brought to you or have not brought. You should keep in touch; then I can advise you."

I said I know that she is busy and I don't want to waste her time. She looked at me very compassionately and said, "I can tell you when I am busy. I must do certain things before I die. It is true. But I will tell you."

She spoke about how identified we are with our body. "Only if we develop a second body, we will not need to keep coming back to the level of the physical body." She wondered if I had been present at the meditation for Madame Lannes. I said I was very struck by what she had said there: how we can free our teachers from the necessity of returning to lower levels. She asked me many questions, as if she was determining whether I had heard what she had said.

Then she spoke about effort and letting go. She said, "Watch for the point in working when it is necessary to let go. Something has to be abandoned. Ego makes the effort, but one comes to a point when the ego has to be passive. The point of transition is subtle. There can be too much effort or too little."

London, May–June 1981; Paris, June 1981.

Remarks of Madame de Salzmann

Link between Two Levels

What religions call God is the higher level, above the mind, but understood through a higher part of the mind. Man is made to create a link between two levels, to receive energy from a higher level in order to have an action on the level below—not a reaction. As long as the ego is dominant, nothing is possible.

❖

There are no miracles. It is all a play of forces.

❖

One needs to find a more active attention that can overcome the passivity. Then a real inner action will take place; and thus a transformation.

❖

There is no loneliness. Everything is in relation with other levels. If the energy of the body is not related to something higher, it will be taken by something lower.

❖

Impressions are the most important thing. It is not easy to receive impressions without reacting.

❖

In order to be related with a higher level, some freedom is necessary from the level of existence where one is. Passivity of the body and of the mind stands in the way. The process requires active attention.

❖

The important thing is to be. If there is no real I, then the ego takes over. Energy cannot be without relationship. If it does not serve I intentionally, then it automatically serves the ego.

❖

The world needs certain vibrations which are produced only when some people work intentionally.

❖

In the beginning, for a long time, one reads, discusses ideas, practices Movements, works with other people, and many other such things. Then comes a time when that is not enough. One needs to understand directly what it means that the centers are not connected. Ideas cannot give the necessary energy. The higher part of the mind needs to be connected with the body.

❖

It is necessary to develop the ability to have an action on the ordinary level.

❖

Religious people talk about the Lord, Seigneur. That is an energy of a very high level. They say, "The Lord helps me." That is true. But something is required of me. I have to prepare myself for this Seigneur to help.

❖

Man can serve the Earth by becoming a link between two levels. He can receive energy from a higher level in order to have an action on the level below; not a reaction.

❖

Unless one prepares others to take one's place and to occupy one's level, so that the right kind of vibration or energy is produced, one is not free to continue one's work in higher spheres. The best way to express our gratitude to our teachers is to work so that they do not have to come back to lower levels. If they are freed from the Earth, they can continue their work at higher levels. Otherwise, they are obliged to return and keep working here.

❖

Ideas alone cannot change a person. Real transformation is brought by the higher energy—from above the head—coming into the body and acting on it. There is resistance, completely lawfully. Gradually, the body will recognize that this transformation is good for him too. Then he will cooperate. He should be given what he needs, not necessarily what he wants.

❖

Watch for the point in working when it is necessary to let go. Something has to be abandoned. Ego makes the effort, but one comes to a point when the ego has to be passive. The point of transition is subtle. There can be too much effort or too little.

❖

Everything Is There in the Body

I am already restless. Ten or twelve days in a strange place with unfamiliar people seems to be my limit. Here I am near the center of the Work, but I am counting the days until I can leave. When I am not here, I am eager to be here. How can it be that when I am here, I want to go away? I miss my familiar routines and intimacies, but when I come to myself, I am clear that I need to be here. When I see this, I experience a remorse of conscience and I wish to work. I feel this physically in the solar plexus.

I see more and more how little I know and how small I am inside. So often I waste opportunities where I could learn something real. It seems as if I have to spend a certain amount of energy in worrying and going over things again and again, otherwise I do not know what to do with this energy. I wish to be important, but I also need to be useful. Something has to depend on me. I realize that violence, both internal and external, arises from a feeling of not being needed, not being useful. But it is clear that on any large scale no particular person is necessary. Even on a small scale, I am not really needed. Everything in the world can go on without me. So a new way of seeing the situation is required. What is my real function? Where am I really needed? Not that myself is needed; but myself as a certain conglomeration of energy, talents, type. What is the right function—that is, for a higher purpose—that myself can serve? Myself, my ego, does not have to be important. In fact, self-importance is the greatest obstacle to development. It is clear that without my ego nothing can be done by me, but when the ego is in charge without making room for others, the intelligent and right order is reversed. The ego is a good servant, but a bad master.

Sometimes I seem to be more interested in being special than in being. Why? There are all kinds of hidden motivations, agitations and apprehensions. Fear seems to be fundamental to my world. It brings deep-seated tensions and resistance to working and I wish to be free of it. Is this a wish for self-improvement? Dr. Welch has often said, "The Work is not a self-improvement society." In my own case, the effect of this remark is to make me lazy and to provide me with more excuses not to work. He often makes fun of the attitude, "If it doesn't hurt, it can't be the work," but I feel more and more that, at least for me, if it doesn't hurt, it really couldn't be the work. Something in me, perhaps the ego, indeed has to be hurt or challenged for it to be the work.

I realize how lazy and imprecise I can be. It was clear in the Movements class this evening. Madame de Dampierre put me in the first row, and she corrected me many times. I have been thinking of the remark in *Revelation* to the effect that 'because I love you, I chastise you.' She said she is surprised how out of touch with my body I am, particularly for an Indian. She seemed to know where I needed help and she asked me to come to an extra class of hers.

❖ ❖ ❖

Madame de Salzmann said, "Everything is there in the body; but we do not realize it. For that it is very important to reach a quiet state, to relax. But one cannot directly try to relax. If I remember my inner aim to be present to myself, then I become aware of my tensions. Then something lets go in a fundamental way."

She spoke with a great deal of power. I was even uneasy looking at her for long. I have been more and more feeling my density and the difficulty of working. How I spare myself! Something is felt, but I don't want to stay in front of that. And I dream again. Oh, the labyrinthine ways of the mind and the heart! Somehow, in the midst of all my confusion and heaviness, I remembered some lines from the *Bhagavad Gita*:

Renouncing all actions to me, mindful of your deepest self
Without expectation, without egoism, struggle without agitation.

How beautiful these words are, especially in Sanskrit. And how difficult to practice! But somehow the words of the Gita are always relevant and useful. I need to remember what this extraordinary book says. It is a different expression of Gurdjieff's injunction: "Remember yourself always and everywhere."

Paris, May-June 1981.

What Is I?

I have just finished presenting my talk on the *Bhagavad Gita*, which Michel had invited me to give at the Paris Foundation. Many senior people in the Work were there, and the whole evening was very intense. I have never addressed an audience with a higher quality of attention. Until today I had not quite understood that attention could be substantial. Madame de Salzmann sat to one side; so I could not look at her without ignoring the others. But a friend said later that for much of the evening Madame had the most seraphic smile on her face. Almost towards the end of the talk, as I was saying something about Krishna's remark, "If I do not work, these worlds would perish," Madame de Salzmann spoke, suddenly and with great intensity, "*I* will work. What is *I*?"

She has so often started a meditation with the words, "*Qui suis-je?* Who am I?" And this is the very formulation of my own question to which I have frequently returned. Here it was: not a question in a book, not her question or my question, but *the* question; the question of a fish on a hook. I understood something and found myself saying things which I had not ever thought about earlier. More than anything else, I was struck by the enormous importance of *yajña*. It was clear to me, even if I could not rationally explain it, that *yajña* is the heart of any spiritual discipline. The usual translation of this as 'sacrifice' is not quite adequate. I understood that it is much to do with an exchange of energies between levels. Many years earlier I had read the remark of a great sage in the *Rig Veda* that "*Yajña* is the navel of the world, around which the whole cosmos turns." Until now I had not understood what this meant. Now it seemed true and obvious.

All this flashed through my mind without taking any time. I could not maintain that level of clarity for long and returned to quoting the scriptures. I expanded a little on the difference between Arjuna saying, "*I* will not fight" and Krishna saying, "*I* work." Madame de Salzmann again said, "*I* will not fight. What *I*? There is something they are not saying. They don't want to tell maybe." I waited, trying to be recollected rather than attempting to recall what I had read. I understood the difference between remembering myself and remembering a quotation. There was a great charge and excitement in the room. After what seemed like a long silence, it became clear to me that here was an occasion for me to hear rather than to speak. I handed the whole question back to her and asked, "How would you put it?" She gave a big smile, and said very mysteriously, "I have my way." That was the end of a very intense exchange, and the tension in the room broke.

Later, Michel wondered if I was reading too many Work ideas into the *Bhagavad Gita*. I said I was no doubt affected by the Work, but it is all there. He said it was good to start an exchange and that it will be useful to continue this next year.

Afterwards, when we stood up, Madame de Salzmann said, "It was very interesting for them what you brought. Also what you say about your scriptures and the Work ideas is right. There have to be many things in common. If you don't take it this way, they will take it another way anyhow."

Later in the conversation, she said, "In London something quite intense was touched in the Movements. They understand the importance and the source of the movements." After a pause, she added, "I will let you know when I go to New York, maybe October or November. You can come there for a little while. It is good you came here."

I learned later that she had come to the talk directly from the airport, having just returned from London. Amazing!

I left Paris the next morning. Michel took me out for a grand breakfast at Hotel Napoleon. As I was leaving, he said, slowly and gravely, "We will keep you in Paris." Then from his briefcase he pulled out a box of chocolates and said, "My Mother has sent this for you."

I left Paris with much food, considerable regret, and some relief. I took a train from Paris to Brussels: the whole journey was occupied with a sumptuous lunch as only the French can do it. I had been invited to a conference on Philosophy of Science which was held at a fifteenth-century monastery at Corsendank in Belgium. This place was now owned privately by the wife of the president of the National Bank, who had all the expensive casualness and simplicity of the very rich. The monastery had undergone an involutionary change: a bar had been installed at the end of the cloisters where a chapel used to be.

About twenty of Europe's important intellectuals were invited, each with much intelligence and vast learning and many languages. I was there largely because the organizer of the conference felt she owed me an academic favour. I mused to myself that England has been well repaid by the United States: English was not the mother tongue of anybody there, but it was still the language of the conference! A pretty waitress whom I had complimented said, "Amuse your dinner." Indeed! There was much food and wine and conversation, all of as high a quality as I can ever recall. The hostess was under the impression that I had just flown in from Canada and she was very solicitous. She tried to be very convivial and amusing, while I tried to 'amuse my dinner' according to the good wishes of the waitress. But it all seemed flat. My heart and soul were just not there. Everything appeared very bizarre, as if I had come from another planet. The natives had amusing rituals and interesting gestures, but I could not get interested in what they were saying.

I kept coming back to what Madame de Salzmann had said—'*Qui suis-je?* Who am I?' I had had this question so long myself. Fellow students at the university used to call me 'Who-am-I Ravindra', but until last evening I had not understood the meaning of the question. It is obvious that this question cannot even be approached in the usual state of consciousness. One needs to be a little transformed in order to ask this question properly. It is clear that whatever I say, whatever I think or read, is not fundamentally going to transform me. Only a higher energy can have an action below. Vision, experience, suffering! Unless I suffer what I am, nothing will change. I say that I am interested in something very high. A very high payment is needed for that. Am I willing to undertake the *yajña* that is needed?

The whole universe could hardly be organized for my glory or importance. I must understand and perform *yajña*—sacrifice and exchange of substances. Intensity and fire! *Yajña*, with 'me, me, me' as the oblation.

Who am I?

Paris, June 1981; Corsendank, June 1981.

When the I Appears

It is clear that one needs to avoid the temptation of manipulation, especially of what is higher. The higher, if it is truly higher than oneself, cannot be manipulated. Trying to manipulate what is higher is a form of violence against oneself, for in the process one is closed off and is not available to the higher energy. Most of our efforts border on manipulation and violence, except when undertaken with great sensitivity and with a sense of sacrifice and service. I remember Madame de Salzmann saying that it is necessary to understand effort as well as letting go. What needs to stay? And what needs to let go? She said, "Watch for the point in working when it is necessary to let go. Something has to be abandoned. Ego makes the effort. One comes to a point; then the ego has to be passive. The point of transition is subtle. There can be too much effort or too little."

There is always the razor's edge: laziness and passivity on one side and manipulation and violence on the other. Either one takes one's rest and says, "Let someone else do it!" or one wants to storm the gates of Heaven with one's ego intact and in charge. It seems so important to distinguish between the 'ego' and the 'I'. It is clear that one needs to be both a warrior and a lover, in different directions and at the same time. Sad is the plight of those who love darkness and struggle against the rising of the Sun. Active receptivity is needed, not a passive agitation. As Madame de Salzmann often said, "No energy can be without relationship. If one is not related upwards, one will be taken downwards and fragmented. The important thing is to be. If there is no real I then the ego takes over."

I wrote to Madame de Salzmann towards the end of the summer of 1981:

I have been trying to work as you had suggested. More and more, I discover deeper and deeper tensions and fears seated in my organism, as if I was almost wholly made up of these fears and anxieties. Also of desires. I notice, however, that I am much more interested in what seems to me to be a positive action, that is, how to be related with a level of energy which is a little higher, rather than being sad about and consumed by the level of my manifestation. I realize how difficult it is to express myself intelligently in a letter, and how much I need to be closer both to myself and to you. I shall come to New York when you are there and next spring–summer again to Paris. Please do let me know when you expect to be in New York. I see how easy it is to be taken by external action and organization. I understand how important these are, but I seem to be unable to keep them in their right place. They take all my attention and I behave like an automaton. Many more observations and insights are floating around in my mind. But I am not sure of their relative merit or depth. I shall wait until we meet in New York to express them.

Her reply came soon:

I was glad to receive your letter and see that your stay in Paris has been of real help to you. I understand what you tell about your difficulty. It is always like that to begin with. We will need to meet when I come to New York. It will probably be beginning of November. I will let you know exactly the date when it will be right for you to come.

I could not go to New York until a few months later, when I had several meetings with her. She very much emphasized the necessity of bringing the energy of the mind and the energy of the body into contact with each other. For these two energies or forces to come together, to make love with each other, the neutralizing force of seeing is required. Then, from the active force of the mind and the passive force of the body, something new can arise. This new, higher level of energy does not become available unless there is a proper order in the lower levels; that is, an integration of the lower parts is essential for an integration with the higher parts.

Madame de Salzmann said, "You try to work. If you are disconnected, stay in front of the lack of connection, or in front of heaviness or sleep. That staying is voluntary suffering. That is the most important thing. Work for an hour or so, then do something simple and contained. You need to practice to be active in life while maintaining the connection between centers."

She emphasized that the body needs to be in the right posture and completely relaxed in order for one to be free of it. Otherwise, in general, the body controls us completely. One needs to break the hold of the body. Ask it to cooperate; punish it, if necessary; give it half of what it wants. In Paris she had said, "Give the body what he needs, not what he wants." Control of the body is necessary. In response to a question of mine, she indicated that she was not too keen on fasting, but suggested eating less. "Eat half of the usual amount, and see." She had similar advice about sex. She said not to be concerned with it now. "The work takes a lot of sexual energy. When it is needed, it will be taken. Meanwhile, it can serve something else." She asked then if I was getting 'thicker'. I soon realized that she meant 'fatter'. She advised me to watch that. "It is an indication of something weakening in one."

I wondered if self-importance, which is really ego-importance, is the energy and the wish for real Self-importance gone awry? It seemed clear that to remember myself is really to re-member the dis-membered self. The Self is not ego. Self-realization is not ego-gratification. Why did I come into existence? It is a wish to be. To be is the very *raison d'être* of coming into existence. To cut myself off from being is to undo the whole point of existence. It is not surprising that both in the Old Testament and the New Testament 'I AM' is the most sacred name of God.

I asked Madame de Salzmann how to distinguish I from ego, and how to struggle against the ego. She said, "Unless there is the I, there is only the ego. So let it be. One recognizes the presence of I from the fact that I wish to serve. Ego does not wish to serve. But until there is the I, let the ego be. It can be useful. What else are you going to do? When the I appears, the ego automatically loses energy and becomes unimportant. It can still be there but it is not in control."

❖ ❖ ❖

In a group meeting, Michel de Salzmann said that the higher needs to act on myself. This is more important than myself making efforts and the like, as Ouspensky emphasizes. The latter is more exoteric, it is alright in the beginning, but not later. Ouspensky does not talk about sensation, movements or attention. So the Work may become too psychological. Now something new is needed: receptive attention rather than active effort or wrong super effort.

In another meeting with Michel, I mentioned to him that I was thinking of writing on *ahimsa*, non-violation, and *yajña*, sacrifice and exchange of energies between levels. He said he has been much interested in non-manipulation, and how to let the higher have an action upon oneself. This is where he feels that an emphasis on effort, super effort, and such can be misleading. Sacrifice of one's ego-self allows an exchange with higher levels. This is the real issue of effort; it can not be spoken about but needs to be practiced in response to a conscious demand.

❖ ❖ ❖

I went to meet Madame de Salzmann again today, even though I felt I did not deserve this meeting. I did not really have a question and I had not worked since the last meeting with her. There was something compulsive about my going to meet her; I just could not stay away. Even she wondered whether after our previous meetings, and the meetings with Michel, I still needed to see her. I did not know. I wonder if an iron filing knows why it is drawn to a magnet. She was, as always, very generous. Meeting with her makes it entirely clear that one needs to work. For that, intentional suffering and conscious labour are needed. Without conscious work, the Earth will be in great danger.

Madame de Salzmann said, "Dying to the old self is necessary for a new birth."

My feeling was deeply touched. What does the 'old self' mean for me? Charming old self, thinking about this or that and desiring one thing and another. I saw that thinking is a form of manipulation, and that desire arises out of fear. The old self is the sum of all of my fears and desires, thoughts and knowledge, the whole mode of relating to everything and everyone. Dying to myself would certainly be death. I shuddered. I reassured myself of the validity of my connection with the world. I was not eager to say adieu.

A bird in a cage.
    Its door wide open.
With no practice in flying,
    Sitting in the cage,
Composing an ode
    To freedom.

London, June 1981; New York, February 1982.

Even Angels Have Egos

Q*ui suis-je?* Who am I?" Madame de Salzmann began the meditation sitting today with this question. It seemed so right, so appropriate and to the point. This is, after all, the question. This is the heart of the matter. There can be no theology or cosmology without autology. How can one measure anything without having an instrument to measure with? And without knowing what the instrument measures? Meister Eckhart said that the soul is as infinite as God, and that there is no way to God except through the soul. It seems true.

I ask myself, "Why do I want to see Madame de Salzmann? Is it vanity? Why do I wish to have a private meeting with her? What do I really need?" I see that I lack intensity. With Madame de Salzmann there is passion. She demands this, both of herself and of others. She is too old now, and too distant, to be interested in social courtesies or anybody's tender feelings, except when it serves what she is needed. With her, I am cornered. I cannot play my usual tricks: I can neither charm her nor convince her of the usefulness of my intellectual formulations. In her presence, either I burn and suffer—and sometimes something is purified in the process—or I make excuses and she suffers, listening patiently without losing hope. Often, I realize later how I spared myself and added to her suffering, losing an opportunity to pay for my existence.

❖ ❖ ❖

I presented myself to Madame de Salzmann upon my arrival in Paris, on what now seems to be my annual pilgrimage for a few weeks. It is really difficult to believe that a person like her exists and is available for us to learn from directly. She was, as always, very generous. She thought I should especially work in the movements. She also said that I need to continue working with others in quiet work, doing small, contained movements at the end. She very much emphasized the attitude of the body. It should not be automatic, but it should be completely relaxed. She said, "At present keep doing your work with others, and also your professional work, giving lectures, writing papers and books. When you need, you disappear for a little while and be by yourself. It is harder to work by oneself, especially at present."

Later, she added, "Conscious suffering is the most important thing. Stay in front of the lack."

She said, "Mr. Gurdjieff said, 'Die to yourself.' That does not mean to die. It means to die to all one's habits."

I saw that I am my habits. And if I die to my habits, I die up to the level of those habits. Therefore, I am free of that level. Liberation and dying to my habits are the same thing.

I know that to go to a meditation sitting or a group meeting or a Movements class is to participate in *yajña*, an exchange of energies requiring a sacrifice of something. All the forms of the Work are invitations to suffer intentionally. I am sure that the responsible people in the Work suffer more than others. That is almost the meaning of responsibility. One can certainly feel this about Madame de Salzmann. The point is not to suffer stupidly and unconsciously.

❖ ❖ ❖

In a men's group this evening, Madame de Salzmann very much emphasized the importance of the right posture. "Your body does not permit the right relationship between centers," she said in general. She herself sits straight and relaxed, illustrating the right posture and a connection with the higher energy.

It seemed obvious that we need to learn how to sit and stand and walk rightly. Theoretically speaking, it is possible that we could be related with a higher energy in any posture, right or wrong. I remember meeting Madame de Salzmann once when she was not sitting in her usual posture. I suppose I must have looked askance for she said, pointing to her 'wrong' posture, "I can sit like this and still be connected, but you cannot."

It is clear that I need all the help I can get. I must not excuse myself, nor must I imitate those who sit without maintaining the right form. I need the correct posture, just as I need the various rules and regulations. They provide help. Madame de Salzmann said that body posture is all. "If the ankle or the arm is one way rather than another, the connection is lost, and the higher energy cannot pass." I recalled reading that a similar emphasis on the posture was placed by the great Zen master Dogen.

After the meeting, Madame de Salzmann asked me to come to her room. She wondered if I understood what she had said in the meeting. I said I had been working according to her instructions in the meeting. She said, "Not quite! Try to work this way and we shall talk about it. Call me tomorrow."

❖ ❖ ❖

The donkey is willing but the monkey is not. It does seem to me, and I told this to Madame de Salzmann during my next meeting with her, that in meditation sittings the body is more cooperative than the associative mind. I told her that I found the mind more troublesome than the body. She said that I see the resistance of the mind but not of the body, but that the body is even more resistant.

Of course, the whole thing, including the mind, may be the 'body'. I get the impression that Madame de Salzmann includes everything that belongs to the level of the Earth as 'body'. This is a slightly different usage than what I am accustomed to. But this is how St. John the Gospel writer uses the word 'flesh'. When it is said that "the Word became flesh," it certainly includes the mind, for there is no suggestion that the Word became merely animal flesh.

I wondered if there is a way to help the body? All I think of, sometimes, is punishment or fasting or abstinence, and the like. She did not think that any of these especially helped if they are not related to work. She said, "Conscious suffering is the most important thing. Religions and traditions have devised all sorts of postures and practices for suffering; but then they forget why."

❖ ❖ ❖

I was invited to breakfast with Madame de Salzmann and Michel. Michel told me that Gurdjieff would often ask him, "What would you choose: the devil who takes you to God, or the god who takes you to the Devil?" Apparently, Gurdjieff asked this question quite often, and each time one had to come up with a fresh and right answer. I wondered what I would choose.

In the general conversation I said something about the ego being so trivial. Madame de Salzmann wondered what there would be if there was no ego. She said, "When real individuality is there, the ego finds its proper place. For some people, Mr. Gurdjieff used to advise them to develop their ego because they were too weak. Then later, when it is not needed to be the master, he would ask them to soak it in cold water."

By 'ego' she seems to mean everything that is personal. I see that it is necessary to make a distinction between the personal and the individual. Self-realization is not myself-realization. The Self worthy of realization is not personal. However, without a definite form or order to the energy there can be no responsibility and no action can be undertaken. Thus individuality (or real I) would require definiteness and an ability to act and to take responsibility. It cannot be said that Jesus Christ was ruled by his ego, but even he needed to become embodied in order to undertake his Father's work. Freedom from the ego is not loss of individuality, otherwise an enlightened soul would not need to live and could simply die. Why does the Buddha need to teach? Surely, he has nothing to gain for his personal benefit.

Is the world a mistake? Is the purpose of one's incarnation merely to escape from the world? Should one simply become spirit without differentiation? Madame de Salzmann so often emphasizes the necessity of action in the world. The real question is how to engage in purposive action without self-interest, and, more importantly, without egoism? How to be a self without being selfish? How to find a centered self without becoming self-centered?

One needs to be really clear about the difference between the personal and the individual. Hindus often go beyond the merely personal, but also beyond the individual; they aspire to remain in *samadhi* without action. Christians, wishing to retain individuality and wanting to save their own souls, often become merely personal. Neither the big Self (the real I) alone nor the little self (the ego) alone will do. At any level, a combination is needed. Then the individual self acts as a lens to focus and gather the energy of the Sun of the Self for the maintenance of proper order in the world. The need is neither for the one nor for the other, but for a right relationship between the two. This is true for all levels. As Madame de Salzmann said, "Even angels have egos, of finer substance. And they have the same difficulty in keeping the ego in check as human beings do."

Paris, April–May 1982.

Unless the Body Is Available

Almost all effort comes from the ego and therefore naturally has an element of manipulation, possessiveness and violence inherent in it. True non-violence, which is not to be confused with lack of force, is obedience to the right order. In the right order, the higher calls and the lower responds. It is necessary to make efforts, even super efforts, for as Krishna says, "Action is better than inaction." But these actions are relatively exoteric. What is important is to let the higher act on oneself. Doing cannot lead to being; action must follow from placing oneself in the right order. The first principle of true ecology is non-violence, that is to say, non-violation of the right order.

I read in all the myths and the sacred literature of the world that the dragon which needs to be tamed has my own face. I know it to be true but somewhere deep down I do not accept this simple fact. The right order leads not to freedom for myself but rather to freedom from myself. But the ego asserts itself and I wish to be important. I have difficulty accepting truth on its own terms; in one way or another I wish to possess it. Though I cannot be sure of her exact words, I recall Madame de Salzmann saying, "That which is true cannot be mine; that which is only mine cannot be true."

❖ ❖ ❖

Madame de Salzmann spoke again about the descent of the higher energy. "Higher energy is there but cannot come down unless the body is available and in equilibrium, without tension. When a connection among the centers is made, the energy comes down the spine." One practices the sensing of the limbs and torso in order to prepare these channels along which the higher energy may descend.

Madame de Salzmann has been placing a lot of emphasis on the availability and equilibrium of the body, so that a connection with the higher energy may be made. She said simply, "*Sans cette rélation, vous n'avez pas de sens.*" ("Without that relationship, you have no meaning.")

I have been trying to understand the effect of such remarks and ideas. Surely, any true insight or great idea comes from above, from a level which I do not ordinarily inhabit. How can my ordinary mind comprehend it? What happens in me is that I am touched at some unaccustomed place for an instant. Then, a flood of associations and explanations takes over, and all sorts of embellishments and exaggerations take place. The result is that the simplicity and directness of the idea or the insight are lost. I see that in this sphere the riches are traps; austerity and poverty seem closer to truth.

What action does an idea have? This seems to be the central issue. We can discuss the Law of Three or the Enneagram, or whatever else and, of course, we need to understand these concepts; but unless an idea causes an inner movement, any talk about it can have little real meaning.

Madame de Salzmann asked something very simple and very important last Sunday in the large group: "You have been in the Work for some years. What difference has it made in your ordinary life?"

That indeed is the question. I must ask, "What action does the Work have on my life?"

I see more and more how little I work. How can I really understand intentional suffering?

❖ ❖ ❖

Again and again Madame de Salzmann emphasizes, "Everything is there in the body. The connection depends on the availability of the body. You must demand something. One has to become really familiar with one's resistance, of the body and of the mind."

I reported to her that I realize more and more how lazy I am, in all the centers. Only in physical work of some sort can I find sufficient engagement and work by myself. Elsewhere, in all activities, I need other people. In fact, I come alive only when there are other people. Writing for me is very difficult; it is too solitary and too intellectual. She said simply, "It is necessary not to give in to passivity. You do not know what you are."

❖ ❖ ❖

Madame de Salzmann was very strong in the group meeting. "The Lord, the *Seigneur*, is there, but he needs my body to come. The body is not ready. It needs to be prepared. If the mind and the body are connected, then the higher energy, which is what religions call *Seigneur*, will appear."

I had an impression of a literal physical conduit between the head and the rest of the body.

She continued: "It cannot be done easily or cheaply. But it must be done. It is necessary for the maintenance of our world. The body has to serve something else, not itself. The body itself is designed for destruction; it has to serve something else."

Afterwards, when I was with her alone, I asked about the willingness to pay. Yes, I find myself willing to pay, in energy, time and money. But something stands in the way. Perhaps it is the Devil who demands to know whether effort is something of the ego. She said, "You have to see. How else would you know? You have a devil. Everyone has a devil. He does not wish to work and finds all sorts of excuses. Look and see."

Paris, May 1982.

The Ego Does Not Wish to Serve

Everything is there in the body; but we do not realize it. For that it is very important to reach a quiet state, to relax. But one cannot directly try to relax. If I remember my inner aim to be present to myself, then I become aware of my tensions. Then something lets go in a fundamental way.

❖

No energy can be without relationship. If one is not related upwards, one will be taken downwards and fragmented. The important thing is to be. If there is no real I then the ego takes over.

❖

Unless there is the I, there is only the ego. So let it be. One recognizes the presence of I from the fact that I wish to serve. Ego does not wish to serve. But until there is the I, let the ego be. It can be useful. What else are you going to do? When the I appears, the ego automatically loses energy and becomes unimportant. It can still be there but it is not in control.

❖

Dying to the old self is necessary for a new birth.

❖

Mr. Gurdjieff said, "Die to yourself." That does not mean to die. It means to die to all one's habits.

❖

If the ankle or the arm is one way rather than another, the connection is lost, and the higher energy cannot pass.

❖

Conscious suffering is the most important thing. Religions and traditions have devised all sorts of postures and practices for suffering; but then they forget why.

❖

Higher energy is there but cannot come down unless the body is available and in equilibrium, without tension.

❖

Everything is there in the body. The connection depends on the availability of the body. You must demand something. One has to become really familiar with one's resistance, of the body and of the mind.

❖

The Lord, the Seigneur, is there but he needs my body to come. The body is not ready. It needs to be prepared. If the mind and the body are connected, then the higher energy, which is what religions call Seigneur, will appear.

❖

It cannot be done easily or cheaply. But it must be done. It is necessary for the maintenance of our world. The body has to serve something else.

It Is Important to Work Now

Madame de Dampierre asked me what I had found of importance during my stay in Paris. I told her, "Quiet work and Movements. I see the heaviness of the body and the imagination of the mind. I see more and more that my body is not tuned." I was a little surprised to hear her say again something which Madame de Salzmann had also said, that I have a very sensitive body. That is surely not what I feel. I see myself as very heavy and stupid, like a large gorilla in a prison of my habits and lethargy. Madame de Salzmann has often said that everything is there in the body. Sometimes I even sense that, but I do not take any real care of it. My body is not tuned; perhaps my mind is, maybe even my feelings are to some extent, but not my body. In any case, there is a lack of connection between the head and the body.

I so often feel trapped in my inanity; ordinary pleasures and ordinary desires and ambitions seem to be all I have, all I am. Often it seems as if I have resigned from even trying to understand the meaning and purpose of my life. Is this what Madame de Salzmann means by seeing one's passivity? If somebody who is significant to me, Madame de Salzmann or Mrs. Welch, tells me something about myself, I am interested for a moment, but then I have doubts, explanations, theories and I go around in the same circles again. How can I die to my own prison, a prison of my acquiescence if not of my own making, a prison of my habits?

Madame de Dampierre said that my work now seems to be getting more concrete. "Now you are in galoshes," she said. "Because you are aware of your situation, you must work."

I hope so. But also, I fear.

I told Madame de Dampierre that I feel stuck in my head and that I almost feel it should be cut off. She said even when one doesn't think or say a word, one can be stuck in the head. She said, "We have a mind as we have a body. One cannot be without the body or the mind. The mind cannot not think any more than the lungs cannot not breathe. But we need to work with a different kind of thinking. Thinking without words; that is attention. That is the energy of the mind which needs to be directed to the body. Even if one can work hard at it only for half an hour a day, a deep satisfaction comes. Not associative thinking, but deep visionary thinking. That is the importance of giving oneself a task or an aim. The task simply is to maintain, or return to, a connection between the mind and the body. That is where sensation can be most useful."

I told Madame de Dampierre that I do not feel nourished by the study of science or the traditions. She said, "In the beginning it is useful to study traditions so that one sees that Gurdjieff did not just invent his teaching. But now one can let go. Later on, when one understands something directly, one can come back to the traditions."

That is precisely what I feel now. I do not need any justification or approval from the traditions or science. Something is either true or not. It is not so because the *Bhagavad Gita* or the Bible says so. I need to know directly. That is what the work is for me now. That is what I need; and that is what I wish. I need to work concretely, seeing directly. Studying this or that, organizing groups and giving lectures about the Work are second best. Unless I have contact with the higher consciousness, all my activities in the Work are fantasy or pouring from the empty into the void. For this contact to come about, the mind and the body have to be related.

How can anything done by the ordinary mind lead to transformation? I wonder about all these study groups about "the Work and traditions" or "the Work and science," and the like. They make so much more sense for those who already see from a higher point of view, for they can bring the true vision to bear on ordinary realities and affect them. But, from the point of view of an aspirant the question is, "Can these studies bring one to a higher consciousness?" A radical departure from the usual and the ordinary is needed in order to come to a different world. The higher world surely is not an extension or augmentation of the lower world. That is why Krishnamurti sometimes makes so much sense in his insistence that thought cannot lead to Truth. Everywhere, we create a Port o' Monkeys—studying this or that and becoming experts—and forgetting the one essential thing. I need always to ask, "What is the one thing needful to do?" The rest is unnecessary and therefore sinful. Real art must be simple, discarding everything which is not necessary. This must apply to the art of living rightly, and searching rightly, much more than to any other art.

❖ ❖ ❖

I see that the lower mind is the source of the problem, not the solution. How right is William Blake when he speaks of "Reasonings like vast serpents Infold around my limbs, bruising my minute articulations."

I told Madame de Salzmann about feeling trapped in the head, and said that others expect me to use my intellect and invite me to corresponding tasks, thus pushing me more and more in that direction. She said, "Mental things are not so important for you now. You need to work directly, especially in quiet work. Often and long and intensely, and with other people when possible. That is the most important thing now— direct experience of contact with the higher energy. All the other pleasures—food, sex, money, children—will find their place. All the money in the world or fifty children will not open the door."

She spoke about the necessity of sacrifice, of paying the price, mainly by voluntary suffering, by staying in front of my inadequacy. I have never seen her so strong. She was distant and near, demanding and compassionate. She asked me, "Are you willing to pay the price?"

I had such a strong feeling I nearly cried. I wanted to say 'yes', but I could see my resistance and inability. I could see myself wanting something very high without being willing to pay for it. She so much emphasized the importance of working now, in the present moment. "It is important to work now. Now is the only possibility, not later. To realize this possibility something is required from you. Do you see it?"

Madame de Salzmann's exhortation, "It is important to work now" and her visage—stern and strong, but not harsh—seem to have engraved themselves on my memory. I need to demand something from myself, even for my own sake. Otherwise I will be deeply disappointed in myself. Who am I? What is demanded of me? Am I willing to pay the price?

Paris, May 1982.

Ideas Are Not Enough

A few months after returning from Paris, I wrote to Madame de Salzmann:

> As the time I spent with you recedes further, I find myself in more and more confusion. What seemed clear then does not seem clear at all now. A kind of meaninglessness and futility of effort is trying to take hold of my psyche again. In particular, it seems difficult to make a demand on myself. And something in me begins to make excuses more and more successfully. I do not wish to live for a lower call and seem unable to respond to a higher one. Nothing other than the work really interests me, but I find myself not working. I know I must work, but soon I forget, as if I have not even heard of it. I find it a great help to work with others.

This was in the summer of 1982, as more and more momentum was gathering in Paris, London and New York for the making of the Movements film. Madame de Salzmann's reply came in the fall:

> I understand very well the state you speak about. You are in front of a new possibility, but it requires a strong work, a decision, a will which is not easy to maintain. It is a moment when the ideas are not enough. There is a force, a higher one; it is in us, but can have no action as long as our state does not

allow it—as long as our centers are not related. At that stage the ideas do not cooperate, one has to feel the inner inadequacy, be touched, suffer from it and give all one's attention to this inner relation which will open the door to the higher energy. We can work deeply at it when you come. I come specially to prepare the pupils to be able to do the Movements in a new way, so that the film can be a demonstration of a new stage of work.

❖ ❖ ❖

Meeting with Madame de Salzmann was, as always, wonderful. I see more and more the necessity of understanding French, for she has difficulty with the subtle nuances in English, although she hardly needs any language at all. She certainly understands without any words being spoken. And she speaks so directly, almost physically, that I once said to Mrs. Welch that one would understand the weight and essence of Madame de Salzmann's words even if she spoke in Chinese!

She again spoke about the necessity of staying in front of one's inadequacy. To suffer oneself is intentional suffering. These are not her words, but this is how I understood her. The body has to be disciplined, not tortured.

Madame de Salzmann said, "The body does not understand the mind. If the body understands that he also gets something, then he cooperates. He needs to be an instrument. If necessary, one should punish the body. Maybe one says, 'Unless a connection is made, I shall not eat.' Maybe one denies the body some other pleasure."

Madame de Salzmann spoke about two currents of energy. "If one is open to a vertical current, that is what makes the astral body. The other current, the horizontal one, is the energy of the physical body. One current is not at the cost of the other or in the place of the other. Without the vertical current there is no meaning to existence. But without the other current of energy no action is possible in the world. To be complete, a human being must relate with both currents."

She made a gesture with her hands which for the first time made the meaning of the cross come alive for me. She added, "Nobody can do this for another. It will even be dangerous for the other if somebody else does it for them."

Madame de Salzmann asked me to come and see her again before leaving for Canada. Her generosity and warmth are overwhelming. Then she could not recall my name to enter it in her appointment book! It is clear that the name is merely a designation, a matter of convention. To be occupied with one's name and the accompanying self-importance, as I am much of the time, simply indicates an occupation with the appearances rather than with what is real.

I am more and more terrified by the deepening awareness of my debt to the elders in the Work. Seeing Madame de Salzmann's exalted state and extreme compassion, I am beginning to understand why Simon, the son of Jonah, was so struck by his own nothingness in the presence of the Christ. He said, "Move away from me, O Lord, for I am a sinful man."

Madame de Salzmann told of an incident, late in Gurdjieff's life, when she came upon him in a place in Switzerland. He was sitting, looking very sad and discouraged. She asked him: "Are you discouraged because we are not working hard enough? Is there something we don't do?" With great feeling he described his sadness as he conveyed to her the immense distance between what was needed and what was being done. He felt compassion for the pupils, as well as his inability to do it for them. Then he waved to her to go and play the piano.

Madame de Salzmann spoke about this with such vividness and feeling, and with moisture in her eyes, that I instinctively reached over and held her hand. She smiled very warmly. I sensed that she was feeling now what she had remembered Gurdjieff feeling then—the great gulf between what was needed and what was accomplished. I felt my own inadequacy, my nothingness. I saw that I do not undertake what is needed.

Exchange of letters, July–August 1982; New York, December 1982.

If One Did Not Have Vanity

I had been thinking of asking a question in the group meeting when Madame de Salzmann herself articulated it: "Is the work accepting what I am, or struggling with what I am?"

In what followed it became clear that these two are not different things. To accept what I am, to suffer myself, to stay in front of my inadequacy, is to struggle with myself. I do not like what I see and I wish to change it immediately so I will not have to suffer what I am in reality. And I see that I cannot in fact change myself, because I do not have enough depth of seeing. Furthermore, the way I am is the result of the whole of my previous life, much of which I do not see. Therefore I imagine myself already in a transformed state. I can see that imagination and fantasy result from not being able to stay with myself as I am. The energy from even the little seeing that I sometimes have goes into weaving a fantastic scenario rather than into a transformation that might result from the heat of suffering. Whatever else it is, the practice of intentional suffering must surely include suffering what I am.

When I am with Madame de Salzmann I feel that both the deepest part of myself as well as the superficial part are seen. She sees what will help me in the realization of my own deepest need and wish, which cannot be contrary to what is objectively needed. Surely, the deepest part in me, as in everyone else, belongs to the objectively truer realm. What needs to be discovered is the way through which one could serve what is higher. Teachers point the way for us to understand and to follow. I see that hesitation, disobedience and even humility are all assertions of the ego. Sacred action has nothing to do with like or dislike or the possibility of failure or success; it simply needs to be done. Krishna speaks so much of this in the *Bhagavad Gita*.

When one is able to be simple, surely the deepest part of the self is the same as the one which resides in Dante's highest heaven. As he so beautifully said at the end of the *Divine Comedy*,

> Like a wheel in perfect balance turning,
> There my will and desire were guided by Love
> The Love that moves the Sun and the other stars.

❖ ❖ ❖

I asked Madame de Salzmann about the relationship between vanity and fear. I see that they are related, but which one causes the other? Is fear a result of vanity or does vanity arise from fear? I have many questions about this but my attention wanders off when I try to look at the two in myself. On this issue, more than anywhere else, I sense the presence of a force interested in resisting clarity in me. When I spoke in the meeting I was in an unusually good state. I imagine my state was partly helped by the fact that I had undertaken not to eat very much before the meeting, but I cannot be sure of this. Madame de Salzmann's reply surprised me somewhat. She said, "You must write about the Work ideas. This effort is necessary." Then she added, perhaps as an afterthought and a corrective both to my vanity and to fear, "Particularly when you understand a little more."

In that brief moment in which there was a pull from both fear and vanity, and at the same time some freedom from them, I must have been a little more available than usual. She looked at me in depth and for long. Then she smiled and added, "More intensity is needed."

What is afraid is always the ego; it wishes to be liked and admired and fears that it will be disapproved. Furthermore, it is the ego which imagines that I am going to do a good job. It is so clear, and Madame de Salzmann has often said something to this effect, that whatever is true cannot be of the ego, and also whatever is merely of the ego cannot be true.

In another meeting, Madame de Salzmann said that one always has some fear, except in the state in which one is internally connected. As I pondered this, it seemed clear, at least theoretically, that only at the level of the Absolute can one be free of fear and desire. At all other levels, it is a matter of relative freedom. Now this seems obvious and even common-place, but at the time this clarity brought me much internal ease and relaxation. Without the recognition of the principle of relativity, one is bound to have an absolutist point of view, which can only remain a mental idea since the Absolute is not where I am. Thus, I can always completely defeat myself right at the beginning of an undertaking. The idea of relativity is a practical aid in maintaining hope. It may be impossible to be perfect as the Father in Heaven is perfect, but it is possible to take one little step towards the right posture, internally and externally. In practice, the older sister or brother can be a more helpful guide and model than the perfect Father. Of course, it is necessary that the guide be connected with the current of aspiration.

Apropos a question of mine about the ego and the I, Madame de Salzmann asked me where I experience the I. I described the different ways I experience the I, or the seer. To one of these descriptions she said that it is very high energy. Then she added, "One can stay in contact with it all the time."

I told her how fear and vanity stand in my way. She said, "If one did not have vanity, what else would motivate one? When something else comes, vanity, or the ego, will automatically take second place."

New York, December 1982.

The Body Must Obey
Something Higher

I see you still retain some sense of your body. This needs to be developed further," said Madame de Salzmann, in practically the first words she spoke to me on my arrival in France from India. She has often remarked on the sensitivity of my body. This puzzles me, especially when I am aware of my awkwardness in the Movements. What does she mean? Gradually I became interested in understanding what she was referring to rather than simply giving in to some ego satisfaction or mild embarrassment arising from an idea that one should not be pleased with what one perceives to be praise. Slowly I understood that what she means by "a sense of the body" is a subtle combination of an inward attention, a quality of breathing and a bodily relaxation. I have the impression that her remark does not have much to do with me personally. It is more likely a remark about my racial and cultural background. In any case, whatever this sense of the body is, it needs to be developed further, as she said.

I asked her how one might cultivate this further. She smiled as if she was just waiting for my question, and said, "It is not that you do it or achieve it. The ego is always there. One needs to see. To see the need for seeing what I am is the most important thing.

"The most important thing is conscious attention—finer and finer, stronger and stronger."

Then she led me, as if by hand, to an attention inward. I had such a sense of connection, mystery and depth, that tears came to my eyes. I sat there with my eyes mostly closed and she sat there looking at me. Next I knew I was recalling that the last time I had felt this intensity of inner connection was in a meeting with her three months earlier in New York where I had gone to see her before leaving for India. She said, "The head is strong. The moment it enters, the connection is lost. It begins to think and comment."

It was clear that the moment was now over. "Call me if you wish anything: to go into any Movements classes or groups or meditation sittings."

I said I shall do what she suggests. I am too often deciding what I need, I told her. I do not know what I need. I have ideas and opinions and a sort of greed about Movements classes and meditation sittings. But I do not know what is really useful for me. She smiled and said that she would see what would be useful and that she would telephone me later in the day. I do not know how anyone can be as generous, compassionate and affectionate as Madame de Salzmann is.

I reflected on my past visits to Paris and my meetings with Madame de Salzmann. I had often realized, usually after my stay was over, how little I hear. I do not really hear or see anything which is radically different from my own ideas and expectations. I am so full of myself, and so convinced that I know what is right that even when I am asking about something, somewhere underneath I am really telling the way it is, or the way it ought to be. Before going to see her this time, I had told myself—as I tell myself now and intend to do every day I am in Paris so that it will sink into my soul—that I am not here to teach or to argue or to criticize and complain. I am here to learn. I need to remember this all the time. When I had initially come to Canada as an immigrant, someone had quite unintentionally taught me a good lesson by saying something to the effect that, 'If you don't like it here, why don't you go back to where you came from?' I suppose I am a sort of temporary spiritual immigrant in Paris; and if I don't like it here I should go back to where I came from. If I already know, I don't need to be here. If I don't know, I need to remember this fact and allow something fresh and new to enter into me.

Madame de Salzmann phoned me later in the day with suggestions for the group meetings, meditation sittings and Movements classes. In effect she wished me to have meetings and classes with all the senior leaders and instructors. Then she said, "Telephone me if you need anything." I saw that in the list of meetings which she had prepared there was only one group meeting a week with her. Already my resolve to be essentially a receptor and not to make demands according to my ideas was in question. I said I wished to have more meetings with her, if she had the time. Without any hesitation she said, "Yes, that is right. You telephone me everyday in the morning to see if we can meet that day. And you come tomorrow at ten."

It is clear that I cannot get away by simply surrendering myself and becoming passive. A continual initiative is needed; yet enough room needs to be left for something unasked for and unexpected.

❖ ❖ ❖

Madame de Salzmann was particularly strong in the group meeting last night. She sat there like a hawk and tiger combined, so much reminding me of some remarkable faces I have seen in pictures of North-American native chiefs of the last century. Suddenly she asked me in French if I understood. I said, "*Oui, madame.*" She demanded, again in French, to describe in detail what it means to me to work. "*Qu'est-ce que vous faites?*" ("What do you do?") It was such a shock. I spoke in English, and she replied in English. Suddenly the whole feeling was different. As if the charmed circle of language, sound and meaning was broken. English sounded flat.

I asked something I have asked earlier and still do not feel clear about: that in my case the problem seems to be less with the body and more with the associative thought. She said, in effect, that one's attention wanders in associative thought, and does not make a connection with the body because the body is full of tensions. The body needs to be perfectly alert and perfectly relaxed. As she says very often, "Any tension anywhere, and the connection is broken.

"The body needs to be disciplined—punished or rewarded—not tortured. It must learn to obey something higher. The body needs to be available.

"Without work, your life means nothing. Without a connection with another level of energy, the work means nothing. If you do not have this connection, you are nothing."

The more strongly she spoke, the more clearly I saw myself in the mirror of my conscience: full of vanity, laziness and habits. However, it was difficult to maintain the requisite intensity to stay there. Soon my mind was thinking of yesterday and tomorrow. I had such a strong feeling in the meeting that it seemed to me it would be inexcusable of me if my children never had a chance to meet her. I decided to ask her after the meeting for a time when I could bring them to meet her, just to see her, for *darshana*.

Madame de Salzmann feels obviously responsible for the people she works with. Expressing the extreme urgency and necessity of work, she wants us to work at least twice perhaps thrice a day. After the meeting she told me that she is going to London in two days. "You can come with me to London, if you like. But, it is better for you to stay here and work in the Movements and in the groups." As on previous occasions when she had gone to London, she added, "You can have me on the phone in London if it is necessary." She had given me some exercises to work on, and wanted to keep an eye on me even from a distance.

After she returned from England, Madame de Salzmann asked me to report what I had discovered from the exercises she had given me. I described my efforts at enduring a physical limitation in the meditation sittings. Past a certain point, something interesting happens, repeatedly. My legs get another shot of energy or sensation, and after a long sitting I can just get up and walk. She was interested in my growing recognition that efforts are necessary to come to a state of no effort. Discipline is needed on the level where one is in order to perceive and receive a spontaneous movement of energy from another level.

Madame de Salzmann asked me many questions, and remarked, "The body must obey something higher; otherwise it has no purpose. It cannot serve only itself."

Paris, March 1983.

Both Effort and Letting
Go Are Needed

The Law of Three is usually presented in terms of active, passive and reconciling forces as if one force is opposed to another and needs to be overcome. All the imagery of battle, resistance, effort, will and the like, arises from that. If applied in this way to male and female energies, what would naturally result is a battle of the sexes. But there are situations when both the forces wish the same, and they are in no way opposed to each other. That is the only occasion when real love-making takes place; only then something new and of a higher quality can arise. Exactly the same applies to the energies of the body and of the mind, if I understand Madame de Salzmann correctly. Only when these energies cooperate and make love to one another can something new arise.

That is also the feeling one has with Michelangelo's painting in the Sistine Chapel: the creation is a result of the coming together of God and man, above and below. I see that this point is not well appreciated in most of Indian spirituality. There is always a wish for freedom from *karma*, from the body, from the whole realm of space–time. What would one do with that freedom? What is liberation for, if not for a right relationship between Heaven and Earth, both within oneself and outside?

I had an extraordinary feeling in this morning's quiet work. There was such a strong and vivid sense of inviting the body, the bride, to a wedding ceremony in which the higher energy is the bridegroom. Different parts are invited to come and participate and to celebrate the union. The field has to be prepared, taken care of and guarded. The thought flashed through my mind that the *Gita Govinda* and the *Song of Songs* sing about this sort of love. The subtle, sensitive, deep feeling is what the new creation is. That is the subtle body or the soul. That subtle body is Mary who can be impregnated by God in order to give birth to the Word.

The ordinary functioning of the head, of the turning thoughts, seems to be the same as that of the ordinary negative emotions and physical tensions: an interference in the process of union. This is where one needs to do battle, and where one needs to be vigilant. The nuptial chamber has to be guarded from intruders. Love-making is subtle and fragile, and a proper quiet place needs to be made and maintained for it.

It is clear that one needs to be both a warrior and a lover. In spiritual writings, sometimes one aspect gets emphasized more than the other, but both are needed. Krishna is both a warrior and a lover. One needs to be a sage-king (*rajarishi*) and one needs to be a warrior-lover (*virapremi*).

❖ ❖ ❖

At a meeting yesterday Madame de Salzmann said, "The Earth needs conscious work. It is in need of higher energy. If I do not let the higher energy descend to the Earth through this body, how else will it come down?"

I had a strong sense of this in the meditation sitting. Just as trees make it possible for a certain kind of energy from the Sun to get down to us, by our work we can assist some higher energies to descend to the Earth. The Earth needs our work, for we can be links or transmitting stations between the Sun and the Earth.

Madame de Salzmann said, "When the relation with the higher energy is there, one does not react. One sees what anybody or anything serves. One does not react to the things inside also. One sees how to make use of the energy which is now being wasted in negative emotions and turning thoughts."

I said to her, "I see that deep down I am very resistant to work and transformation. I am not really interested. I don't see the necessity or the urgency of working. Is it that I don't really see the terror of my situation? I remember Krishnamurti saying to me once, 'Sir, you don't see that the house is on fire.'"

What one constantly needs to be aware of, and always forgets, is that in the ordinary state one is cut off from the Real, from the energy that will give clarity, meaning and sense to one's life. Out of vanity, desire, laziness and fear, one lives isolated from the great reservoir of Being, in an isolated and very small chunk of being called myself. None of one's activities, no honour, no pleasures, mean anything if one is cut off from the only thing that gives any real meaning. Sometimes I have a feeling that I understand what the sage Yajñavalkya said in one of the ancient Upanishads, "It is only for the sake of the real I (*Atman*) that one loves the family or the kingdom, or one's own very self."

There is no point in any learning except that it lead to the Self. I need to suffer the fact that I am not open to that; I am not related to that. The only really necessary thing is more and more availability to the true I. Meanwhile, one needs to live in freedom, not in fear. Nothing real can be understood in fear. The terror of being cut off from the Real is not fear in the ordinary sense. That terror is not of the ego; it arises from a fleeting contact with the real Self that wishes to emerge and needs to be nurtured.

How does one in sincerity work in order to lessen the sorrow of His Endlessness? If this question is not to be merely words and sentimental homily, intentional suffering and sacrifice are needed.

❖ ❖ ❖

I often feel that Madame de Salzmann is saying something new, other than what Gurdjieff brought, although there is a discernible continuity of the teaching. It seems that the emphasis now is not so much on 'effort' as on 'being available' to the higher energy entering at the top of the head. Perhaps now some people in the Work are ready for that. Also, it seems that she has been emphasizing the new aspect only in the last four or five years. She said, "The whole work is being related to the higher energy, and letting it pass through me, even when in movement. The Movements are an aid for that."

On the one hand, one constantly hears in the Work—especially in the writings and talks of Ouspensky and Gurdjieff—about will, effort, conscious labour, intentional undertaking and the like. On the other hand, Madame de Salzmann in particular is emphasizing being available, letting go. In the later stages of meditation, one is not even concerned with the body. There the body is asleep as it were, and it does not change position or demand anything. It is only the fine attention, which has been freed from the self-occupations of the body or the mind, that matters. It is not the posture or breathing or any kind of effort. One might say that a certain kind of forgetting is a part of remembering or being connected with the Real. One needs to understand this in order to be free of one's own will, effort, aim and the like in order to be able to hear and serve a higher aim. As Madame de Salzmann said, "Both effort and letting go are needed. It is important to know the point of transition. It is very subtle. The ego makes the effort, then the ego has to let go. Always search for the balance."

I see that much of the effort is for the purpose of freeing oneself from displaced time. Only then can one be here, now. This 'now' is in time but it is not of time; it refers more to a quality of being. In that sense, one wishes and needs to live in eternity, freed from time. Time and imagination are very intimately connected. Action can be sacred only when it is done from the perspective of eternity, situated in the present.

❖ ❖ ❖

There was a very deep meditation sitting last evening with Madame de Salzmann. I see more and more that one can read a lot and talk a lot and obtain a certain expansion and excitement from great ideas, but one is not transformed this way. Of course, one can leave big ideas aside, and then one is taken by trivial concerns: bills, inflation, daily news or this and that. That is also mechanical. Those who do not think well or clearly are also tyrannized by turning thoughts. How can one be free of the whole level of self-occupation—money, name, food and sex— the entire domain of fear and desire. How can I be free of my very self that is wholly made up of these fears and desires? I see I do not want only theory. I wish to have concrete facts. But am I willing to pay the price? I see more and more that a sacrifice of my self-importance is the price.

Paris, April–May 1983.

Remarks of Madame de Salzmann

Two Currents of Energy

It is important to work now. Now is the only possibility, not later. To realize this possibility something is required from you.

❖

It is a moment when the ideas are not enough. There is a force, a higher one; it is in us, but can have no action as long as our state does not allow it—as long as our centers are not related. At that stage the ideas do not cooperate, one has to feel the inner inadequacy, be touched, suffer from it and give all one's attention to this inner relation which will open the door to the higher energy.

❖

The body does not understand the mind. If the body understands that he also gets something, then he cooperates. He needs to be an instrument.

❖

If one is open to a vertical current, that is what makes the astral body. The other current, the horizontal one, is the energy of the physical body. One current is not at the cost of the other or in the place of the other. Without the vertical current there is no meaning to existence. But without the other current of energy no action is possible in the world. To be complete, a human being must relate with both currents.

❖

The most important thing is conscious attention—finer and finer, stronger and stronger.

❖

The body needs to be disciplined—punished or rewarded—not tortured. It must learn to obey something higher. The body needs to be available.

❖

Without work, your life means nothing. Without a connection with another level of energy, the work means nothing. If you do not have this connection, you are nothing.

❖

When the relation with the higher energy is there, one does not react. One sees what anybody or anything serves. One does not react to the things inside also. One sees how to make use of the energy which is now being wasted in negative emotions and turning thoughts.

❖

The whole work is being related to the higher energy, and letting it pass through me, even when in movement. The Movements are an aid for that.

❖

Both effort and letting go are needed. It is important to know the point of transition. It is very subtle. The ego makes the effort, then the ego has to let go. Always search for the balance.

I Can Awaken Me

Sometimes I see quite clearly the difficulty of working intentionally and my enormous resistance. I seem to be occupied with self-importance and vanity almost all the time. How can I be simple with respect to inner work? How can I stay in front of my inadequacy?

In order to work, it is necessary to have a struggle between the 'yes' and the 'no'. Unless something in me is obliged, against my ordinary self-will, it is not the work. Madame de Salzmann was very clear and emphatic about this.

Today, more than ever before, I realized that a conscious effort of attention is much more important than an effort of the muscles. Perhaps the former is an effort of being, whereas the latter is an effort of doing. One must not denigrate any effort; if there is a purity of intention and a wish to work, any effort, however external and small, is right and useful.

Intentional work (or conscious attention) and voluntary suffering are the keys to the work. If I am not related to the energy which comes from above, I must suffer voluntarily. I must stay in front of my insufficiency and the lack of relationship. If I am related, I need simply to continue working intentionally, with conscious attention. That is all. The rest is mere talk. Being related to a higher level, to the real I, is self-remembering. I am called and I respond. When I am not called, or when I cannot hear that I am called, or when I cannot respond, I suffer.

Last evening at the Maison, the meditation sitting was particularly profound. At one moment I had a strong sensation and I felt that I

was going to pass out. I wondered if it was the heat or the closed room
or something else. I debated with myself whether I should get up and
go out or whether I should just lie down between the rows. I did not
want to disturb others by getting up, nor did I want to make a scene by
passing out there. All this internal discussion did not take long. Finally,
I lay down right there and a wave passed over me and I lost consciousness. I do not know for how long, perhaps for no more than a minute;
then I sat up straight as before and continued sitting with everyone, as if
nothing had happened. But now my mind was exceptionally clear.

I had been sitting rather far from the front and I was convinced
that nobody had noticed that I had to lie down during the sitting. But
at the end of the meditation Madame de Salzmann asked me to see her
in her room. She asked me many questions. Then she remarked that an
energy of a very high level had come into my body and that I was not
prepared for it and could not withstand it. She had noticed that after a
little while I had resumed my posture and continued working. She said,
"You remind me of myself when I was young ..." I was so pleased to
hear this remark; I could hardly imagine a greater compliment. Before
I had much time to savour this bouquet, she added, as if completing the
sentence, "... determined and arrogant."

There I was: suspended between hope and reality, fact and
possibility.

❖ ❖ ❖

In another meeting, Madame de Salzmann said, "It is necessary to maintain a contact between the mind and the body, that is to say, a sensation. That permits an opening for the energy which comes from above
the head. While one is in relationship with that energy there is a sort of
freedom which one can sense. Otherwise, there is always some fear."

Afterwards, during the meditation sitting, I had a very vivid sensation on the top of my head, as if the hand of God was resting there. It
has been said that breathing has a rhythm different from the rhythm of
the energy which comes from above. It is right: the energy is completely

independent of the functions, independent of thoughts, of sensations, of breathing.

I had an image of my interior as a household in which it is possible to create harmony. My ordinary mind and body must come together in sensation. Then there is an attention which can be vigilant so that no disorder arises: no tensions, negative reactions, or mechanical associations. Then, as harmony reigns in the household, the conscious attention can wait at the door of the head. That attention waits upon the Guest who may come from above. The more harmony there is in the household, the freer the attention is to wait upon the Guest. If the Guest comes, the attention accompanies her wherever she goes.

Today, there was a presence; I heard a rose petal fall.

❖ ❖ ❖

Madame de Salzmann said, "The body is not the most important thing. The important thing is the real I, which is independent of the physical body. But the body is very necessary because the higher energy needs the body in order to manifest itself. The body is needed so that the I can have an action. That I can create a new body if the connection is strong enough, that is to say, if one permits the higher energy to pass into me. The conscious response or attention, which arises from the me, which is personal, serves as a thread for connecting the I and the me. The I is not personal. I can awaken me and serve the Earth. The Earth as a whole has need of more conscious energy."

In the presence of Madame de Salzmann one can see the grand scale and the ladder of evolution. By myself, I do not see what the life of the Earth is; nor do I see what my responsibility is in the maintenance and evolution of the life of the Earth. But a part of myself understands. It is necessary that the connection with the conscious energy be strengthened. This requires a very strong and steady effort. One must work for oneself and for the Earth. In this way, one can approach the great Bodhisattva vow to help the evolution of all sentient beings.

❖ ❖ ❖

Madame de Salzmann has been very busy with the film. She had asked
me to telephone her before leaving Paris in order to determine whether
we could meet once again. I called to discover that she has far too many
things to attend to and that she could not see me. So I said goodbye and
she said, "I wish everything good for you. Maybe we will meet later—
sometimes, somewhere."

Never before have I had the feeling that today may be my final
goodbye to her. I was very moved, and I said to myself that it is necessary
to undertake conscious work by myself and understand what she means
by saying, "I can awaken me and serve the Earth."

Paris, June–July 1983.

Maintain an Opening

As the time to leave Paris came closer, I felt an apprehension about returning to Canada. I was sure that I would soon be engulfed by my habits and that nothing would have changed in the group there. Even with all the help I have been given, it could hardly be said that much has been transformed in me. Why should one expect any serious transformation in others? However, I have to return home, for that is where I need to cultivate my own garden.

I see that true freedom is freedom from myself. Myself is nothing but my conditioning, good or bad. The Buddha said, "I have done nothing of my own liking. I am free." I imagine he was free of the whole realm of 'I like this' or 'I don't like this.' He did precisely what he saw needed to be done, whether he liked it or not. But I do nothing that I do not like to do, unless I am compelled by circumstances.

❖ ❖ ❖

I was very struck by a poem of the seventeenth-century poet, Jean Racine, entitled *Plainte d'un Chrétien, sur les contrariétés qu'il éprouve au dedans de lui-même* (Lament of a Christian on the contradictions he experiences within himself). It expressed my situation exactly:

> *Mon Dieu, quelle guerre cruelle!*
> *Je trouve deux hommes en moi:*
> *L'un veut que plein d'amour pour toi*

Mon coeur te soit toujours fidèle.
L'autre à tes volontés rebelle
Ma révolte contre ta loi.

(My God, what a cruel battle!
I find two men in me:
One wishes to be filled with love for you
My heart always faithful to you.
The other rebels against your will
My revolt against your law.)

It so much reminded me of a couplet from the *Mahabharata*:

I know what is right but I do not follow it
I know what is wrong but I do not refrain from it.
You, Krishna, who are seated in my heart
You do with me what you wish.

❖ ❖ ❖

In the summer I tried to work by myself and to test my understanding of what I had heard from Madame de Salzmann. I wrote her a letter in the fall describing my situation and raising some questions:

It was very useful for me to be in Paris last March-July. I have so much missed being near you and working with you. Even though I realize that the wish and the strength for work have to come from deep inside, I seem to need external help from the right sources. Something very deep inside me resists by doubting or by claiming that the whole effort is unnecessary or hopeless. Sometimes I think about the work, and that substitutes for any direct and substantial effort. However, by fits and starts, I continue.

I have one or two specific questions to ask you, so that I can understand clearly. By the 'energy of the mind' I understand 'attention'; by the 'energy of the body' I understand different degrees of 'sensation'. When we speak about 'presence', it seems to me to be a conjunction of attention and sensation which is not localized anywhere, but is distributed throughout the torso. In that state when one wishes to 'open the body and the mind upwards', I seem to experience sometimes a descending of fine energy, from above the head, into the body, especially down the back. In general, the sensation corresponding to this energy animates the whole back and moves up to the abdomen; but it seems to stop there and does not move upward.

Just after I mailed the letter, as I was putting away various notebooks, my journal fell open at the page where I had inquired about the fact that I sense the energy descend in me, but often the energy simply stays there, in the region of my abdomen, and does not re-ascend. Madame de Salzmann had said, "That does not matter. That energy has its own life. Maybe at this moment it has no need to ascend. You must maintain the opening and let the energy have its own movement."

It seems increasingly clear, even obvious, that my body cannot be useful only for itself; it has to serve something higher. And if the body or the mind serves something higher, it cannot dictate to the higher how to conduct itself. The body–mind must listen and obey. That is why it should be relaxed and quiet; otherwise it cannot hear. If it cannot hear, it cannot obey.

Paris, June 1983; Halifax, October 1983.

Until Another Body
Is Developed

When I went in to meet Madame de Salzmann she said, "Ah! I have not seen you for a long time."

I told her what I had discovered with the help of the two exercises which she had given me. She said, "It is necessary to have freedom from the body. One can see that it has its place and function here. Even if I may not need it any more myself I may need to stay in the body for the sake of the others. I need the body until another body is developed. The body makes demands all the time: 'me, me, me'. But when I am connected with a more subtle energy then I don't react as 'me, me, me'.

"That is the most important work for you now: to work for half an hour or so, to connect with higher energy, then, throughout the day, to try to come back to it, to give it more importance than anything else. Even if you cannot be connected, *stay* with the disconnection. This is the most important thing for you to work on." She added, "Just sensation is not enough. One needs a connection with higher energy."

I asked her about the increase in sexual energy which I had experienced during a time period of one or two weeks when the quiet inner work had been strong. Should one try to resist sexual expression? I said I was a little surprised by the increase of sexual energy since I would have expected it to have been used up innerly.

She said, "Sex energy can be used in the work, but only when one is very advanced. At present don't do anything about it, otherwise, one can do something wrong. It is like food and drink. The body needs it and wants it; it is quite right."

Madame de Salzmann told me that the Work is making good progress, especially in some places. As I was about to leave, she asked me how long I had been in the Work. I have no idea what entered into me. I said without any hesitation, "Many life times." As soon as this reply had escaped my mouth, I felt chagrined for having sounded flip and cheeky. She looked at me intently, stopping both my external apologizing and internal considering. After what seemed a long time she said, "That is right. What you say is true." I had the impression of sitting in front of a person who was scanning my previous lives.

In a group meeting later, Madame de Salzmann spoke about the necessity of the connection between the mind and the body. She said, "The whole being needs this connection. When one is connected with something higher, and serving a common aim, then one does not react."

I am clearly not connected with it; I find myself so much in reaction. A phrase from one of the letters of John in the New Testament flashed through my mind. I had read it several years ago and I had at that time thought it to be a nice sentimental homily. Now it was clear that it is a statement of a higher law. I recalled John saying, "We must be touched by the Holy Spirit, for we love one another." If I am not touched by the Holy Spirit, if I am not connected with the higher energy, I do not, and cannot, love others; I simply react.

❖ ❖ ❖

In Switzerland, watching Madame de Salzmann, aged ninety-five, walk down the mountain at Chandolin produced a great feeling of gratitude in me. She does not spare herself in any way, and is always making some demand on herself. Everyone near her is naturally drawn into the circle of effort and search. We all wish to respond to her teaching because we see in her a model.

At the end of the day, and after having, as Michel said, "turned an ordinary camp into an extraordinary one," Madame de Salzmann left. Quite full with the subtle food she had given and somewhat connected with the energy she had demonstrated, we all stood quite amazed watching her walk up the steep mountain path. Suddenly Josée de Salzmann remembered that she had meant to give Madame de Salzmann a piece of a special cake which had been made for her but which had been forgotten in the excitement. I volunteered to run up with the cake. I don't ever recall moving so fast and so lightly. I soon caught up with Madame de Salzmann on the mountain.

A few days later, among the festivities marking the end of the intensive period of work, some people were asked to physically indicate or in some way to re-live the most significant moment or event of the whole period. For me, the most significant event of the week had been the visit of Madame de Salzmann, and I had been happy to have run the cake up the mountain for her. The occasion was full of feeling for me, largely of gratitude, and one in which the body had rightly and lightly played its part. So now I tried to show myself running up the mountain, carrying a piece of cake for Madame de Salzmann.

What I could not show by any external gesture was how strongly my heart had responded to what she had asked me in the afternoon when I had met her on my own: "Why do you live? What is the meaning of your life?"

New York, March 1984; Chandolin, July 1984.

The Fear of 'Not Being Able To'

I am off to New York again. What do I seek? Certainly not an organization which will give me solace and self-importance. I need situations which will not let me rest and which will not allow me to ignore my true aim. I do not know who I am. But I need to know it, and I wish to know it. What is needed from me? So much has been given to me. How can I forget the terrifying law expressed in the Gospels that from those to whom much is given much is demanded?

What is my question now? What is worth asking Madame de Salzmann? Do I really have a serious question? In a way I am done with questions. I see that there is a certain violence in questioning. What I wish to open to is so much above my usual level, and my inquiry imposes my level on it, reducing it. I recall reading Francis Bacon describe the method of scientific knowledge. According to him, scientists cannot and should not listen to nature as innocent children; they should instead be putting nature on the rack and sitting in judgment on her. This sort of inquiry becomes an inquisition. And I see the origin of this attitude in me: it arises from a wish to control what I inquire into. In its turn, the wish to control arises out of fear.

In any case, it does not matter what I ask. There are questions to be sure; but the important thing is to be with her, to see her and to be seen by her. I am nourished by her presence. Just to be with her, to breathe the same air, to work in her presence is much more significant to me than any of my questions, however intelligent or important they may be. My questions keep me bound to my level. I need to listen to the perceptions and insights of Madame de Salzmann, in wonder, and to bear the fact that I do not understand them.

❖ ❖ ❖

Madame de Salzmann looked very tired when I went to meet her. She was clearly so busy: someone had just left as I arrived, and someone else came in as I left.

She is no longer interested in ordinary facts and she no longer remembers ordinary details, but when she speaks about the work she is transformed. I believe that now she is mostly a subtle body living in a planetary body which has become very fragile. I remember her telling me that even if one does not any longer need the body for oneself, one may still continue in it if it is needed for the sake of others. Clearly, others need her presence, and her continued physical existence. I see I need her physical presence for something is not settled in me yet.

I checked with her the details of an exercise which she had given and to which I had had a particularly strong resistance. I asked her how to make efforts in the Work without fear. She said, "The real fear is the fear of 'not being able to'. "

Then she led me, as she has so often, through the exercise of attending to the energy which comes from above and moves into the body. She said this energy relates to the second body. "The second body can stand outside the ordinary body, in front or behind, if it is strong and concentrated. It has its own intelligence. That is possible with the work on attention."

After a meditation sitting, I had an unusual clarity about the movement of energy in the body. I realized that the movement goes on even when one does not pay attention to it, just as breathing continues unattended. However, as with breathing, paying attention changes the quality of the movement. Perhaps this is why there is a great deal of emphasis in the Work on the movement of energy in the body during meditation.

❖ ❖ ❖

Madame de Salzmann was in the New York Foundation on the occasion of the January 13th celebrations. Somewhat unexpectedly, she spoke about Gurdjieff's death. She said, "He called me and said, 'You stay here and watch me go out.' Then his second body left his first body. It was something wonderful; the force was very great. We can develop the second body by working."

I wondered for a few moments why she was telling us about Gurdjieff's death at a time intended to mark his birth. But, then, who knows? Maybe she was talking about a new birth; or maybe she was speaking of her own death. She said she will be a hundred soon.

Madame de Salzmann also talked about maintaining a connection through Henri Tracol and through her son. It seemed like a goodbye to the Americans. I wonder if she will ever come back again.

One of the Movements in the film shown this evening, called "An Expression of Cosmic Order," was very striking. A dancer in the Movement moves into an inner circle and the gates close behind her. She glimpses the level above and turns towards the gates which open. She steps out into the outer circle and the gates close behind her. She brings that vision and energy to the level of the people below. With Madame de Salzmann present, and myself still in the glow of my meeting with her earlier in the afternoon, the whole Movement seemed so true and natural. I have never felt this way about any other Movement. The fact of receiving from above and transmitting below seemed to me to be visible in that Movement.

❖ ❖ ❖

Yesterday, in a group meeting, I asked Madame de Salzmann, "How do I know I am seeing or doing or experiencing what you speak about?" For me this is an important scientific question. I can simply imagine that I am experiencing what she is experiencing and describing. All I hear are her words; I do not really know what she is experiencing. It is a question about communication, objectivity, precision, symbolic use of language and the like. She handed my question to Mr. Tracol who suggested in effect that the important thing is not to find the answer to a question of this sort but to keep the question alive and to deepen it.

Mr. Tracol, who reminds me more and more of a Hindu mystic, wove a subtle middle ground between effort and acceptance. He spoke of the ideas as offers made to us, an invitation to a dance. "The dance is going on; I am invited to participate in it. Not that I try, but something is offered to be tried. I am tried." I have been quite clear for some time that although it is important for me to see, it is even more important for myself to be seen from the vantage point of a higher consciousness. A subtle combination of effort and letting go is needed; one can be not only too passive but also too active at the level where one is.

Mr. Tracol said that Gurdjieff would sometimes very much emphasize one aspect of the teaching. But if the next time someone started with "Last week you said ..." he would dismiss it by saying, "How could I say such a stupid thing?" It is important not to get stuck in a partial vision. Constant vigilance and nimbleness are needed; otherwise one cannot dance.

New York, January 1985.

Very Good Is Not Enough

I have been asking myself, "How can I understand and live the saying, 'When a man awakes he can die; when he dies he can be born?' What must die in me? How can I see that? And how might I die?"

When I met Michel de Salzmann at breakfast, he spoke about the necessity of man number four, on the way to becoming man number five, a real man, receiving and transmitting. I raised with him the question about awakening, dying and being born, and we spoke about it at length. I was very interested in what he said. Rather than emphasizing dying all at once, as Ouspensky did, Michel spoke about the process of awakening in which the little I's gradually die in the big I.

❖ ❖ ❖

When I met Madame de Salzmann, she reiterated the necessity of integrating the energy of the mind and of the body, and of maintaining a sensation. "When one is calm and relaxed one should try to move one's arms or walk a little without losing presence. The body is necessary, but it is not the most important thing. It must obey something else. In fact, the body wants and likes the contact with the energy which comes from above, which comes from God. But we are taken by automatism. One must liberate the subtle body from the prison of habits of the ordinary body."

In the presence of Madame de Salzmann one always senses the greatness of the human purpose as well as the difficulty of fulfilling it.

She recounted having seen on some occasions an expression of suffering on Gurdjieff's face. "He was thinking about the continuation of the Work after his death. Now I understand what he felt. What to do now? How to continue the Work?"

I could feel her suffering. Her responsibility is immense. She looked at me intently for a long time without saying anything. Meanwhile, I was searching inside myself for the level which could respond to the demand. After a while, she said, switching to English, "Mr. Gurdjieff used to say, 'Very good is not enough.'"

I tried to raise a question, returning to French, for I know she feels much more comfortable in it. I said, "I notice that in me the 'yes' and the 'no' are both automatic. I find nothing which is conscious and separate from the 'yes' and the 'no'." She spoke as if she had not heard me, or as if my question made no sense, and said, "It is necessary to make conscious attention stronger."

Madame de Salzmann is entirely incredible! So strong, so practical and without any reaction. When one sees her, one understands what has to die in order for a real birth to take place. She said, "The whole thing is a play of forces, those from above and those from below. And everything is a part of conscious energy."

I grew up as a child hearing statements like this. I had no idea what the grown-ups, or the books they were quoting, meant by such remarks. I suppose somewhere these statements must have left an impression on my psyche. In any case, now they seem not only intelligible but obvious, especially in the presence of Madame de Salzmann. It is so clear that what we understand depends on our state. When we are no longer in the right state we no longer see and we forget even straightforward things which we understood quite well earlier. We are like Bottom in Shakespeare's *Midsummer Night's Dream*: having seen a fairy in an unusual state, when he returns to his usual state he has only a vague memory and cannot say anything. As Puck said, referring to us, "Lord, what fools these mortals be!"

❖ ❖ ❖

Speaking with Madame de Dampierre I raised the question of the effect on the Earth if we do not work. I said that I understand the idea but I do not have the corresponding feeling. Occasionally, for an instant, I am touched by the idea. At that moment, I am full of feeling and pressed by the weight of responsibility. She thought for a few moments and said, "It is good that you don't feel that. Otherwise, in general, it is romantic. Take it simply. The finer energy in me, which comes when one works, has an effect on the whole body, and by osmosis on the Earth. In fact, this idea is not new. Many traditions talk about disaster befalling the Earth if there is a lack of consciousness."

❖ ❖ ❖

It is almost impossible to believe that such a human being as Madame de Salzmann exists. I wonder what is the reason for her to continue living now, except to pass the necessary understanding of the work to anyone who wishes to learn. I should not miss any opportunity to be in her presence. I suppose I am obliged to present my paper at the meeting of the scholars in Montreal which I had agreed to do, but I shall go to New York as soon as I can in order to be with her. For me the whole 'important' conference is not worth a single meeting with her, and I cannot bear the speculations of the scholars of religion after spending some time in her presence. It almost physically hurts me to hear academics speak about subtle aspects of mystical experience or of God and of other realities of which we cannot possibly have any direct experience in our untransformed state.

❖ ❖ ❖

Madame de Salzmann came to the meditation sitting, and her presence created a special demand even though she did not say a word. Afterwards, in the group with Mr. Tracol, she said nothing until the end. She sat there listening. Then she spoke for nearly fifteen minutes. She said, "It is a special moment for the Work now. It is necessary to work more consciously and directly. Without any tension. If you are not related, stay in front of your fragmentation. Stay in front of what you are."

Listening to her, I was sure that we are a link between levels. This is always true. It is necessary to receive and to transmit, and to engage in this exchange, more and more consciously. This conscious exchange, this *yajña*, is not possible without the sacrifice of what is mechanical and unconscious. I understand more and more why a sage in the *Rig Veda* said that "*Yajña* is the navel of the cosmos." Without the right exchange between levels the cosmos will disintegrate.

Paris, May 1985.

Remarks of Madame de Salzmann

Freedom from the Body

It is necessary to maintain a contact between the mind and the body, that is to say, a sensation. That permits an opening for the energy which comes from above the head. While one is in relationship with that energy there is a sort of freedom which one can sense. Otherwise, there is always some fear.

❖

The body is not the most important thing. The important thing is the real I, which is independent of the physical body. But the body is very necessary because the higher energy needs the body in order to manifest itself. The body is needed so that the I can have an action. That I can create a new body if the connection is strong enough, that is to say, if one permits the higher energy to pass into me. The conscious response or attention, which arises from the me, which is personal, serves as a thread for connecting the I and the me. The I is not personal. I can awaken me and serve the Earth. The Earth as a whole has need of more conscious energy.

❖

It is necessary to have freedom from the body. One can see that it has its place and function here. Even if I may not need it any more myself I may need to stay in the body for the sake of the others. I need the body until another body is developed. The body makes demands all the time: 'me, me, me'. But when I am connected with a more subtle energy then I don't react as 'me, me, me'.

❖

The whole being needs this connection between the mind and the body. When one is connected with something higher, and serving a common aim, then one does not react.

❖

The second body can stand outside the ordinary body, in front or behind, if it is strong and concentrated. It has its own intelligence. That is possible with the work on attention.

❖

When one is calm and relaxed one should try to move one's arms or walk a little without losing presence. The body is necessary, but it is not the most important thing. It must obey something else. In fact, the body wants and likes the contact with the energy which comes from above, which comes from God. But we are taken by automatism. One must liberate the subtle body from the prison of habits of the ordinary body.

❖

The whole thing is a play of forces, those from above and those from below. And everything is a part of conscious energy.

❖

It Is the Same in the Workshop as in Meditation

Madame de Salzmann came to the day of work at the Maison and went to all the places—the kitchen, the sewing room, the Movements hall, the library and the workshop. It appears as if she wishes to authenticate all things, all activities and to affirm all those who take responsibility. The work is all this but, she says, "At the same time, what is most important is the connection with higher energy. And when one is not related, one must stay in front of the lack of connection. Stay in front of whatever is taking place: stay in front of your connection or the lack of it. Stay in front."

I feel that '*Restez devant!*', 'Stay in front!', is the mantra which Madame de Salzmann is giving us. It needs to be constantly kept in mind.

Madame de Salzmann came to the workshop where there was a great deal of noise from the saws and the drills. I was struggling with a large piece of wood on the table saw. She came close to me and smiled. Over the din, she said loudly, "Do you see it is the same here as in the sitting?"

Madame de Salzmann's remark arrested everyone's attention and completely changed the atmosphere in the workshop. After she left, my associative mind wondered if she meant that the activity in the workshop is as sacred and as important as meditation is. Or, did she mean that one's mind, my mind, is as noisy during meditation as the noise in the workshop is. I recalled Krishnamurti saying to me, in response to my inquiry about the nature of mind, that his mind was like a millpond. And then he had added with mischievous delight that my mind was like a mill! In the aftermath of Madame de Salzmann's remark, I had a particularly strong impression of my mind just carrying on, associating this with that. But, somehow, I was quite detached from it and could watch the monkey with its antics and be amused by it.

During lunch, Madame de Salzmann must have seen that most of us were not related internally in the way she shows and teaches. She suggested that when we come for a day of work, we are each responsible for bringing a certain energy. She placed a great deal of emphasis on the idea of two energies or forces coming in contact, from above and from below. The energy from above is very important, but in order for it to develop it must come in contact with the energy from below.

❖ ❖ ❖

It seems entirely clear that the really important thing is to see, not to read or to think. I believe it was Wittgenstein who said in a moment of insight, "Don't think; look!" One could even say, "Don't look; see!" Be especially wary of those, both outside and inside each of us, who merely talk and have words about words. It is necessary to be a true scientist of the interior. I am interested in the energy or the attention or the consciousness which is in me, and which passes through me. Surely it is for the sake of that energy alone that one undertakes Yoga or Zen or the Work, and studies the corresponding books and scriptures. It is very necessary to keep the intention clear and not get lost in erudition, pedantry or explanation: one must know directly what is. Many years ago I said to Madame de Salzmann, and I need to remind myself of this again and again, that I wish to have the sort of knowledge which I can touch, which I can eat. Unless my body and soul are substantially nourished by what I see and know, nothing real can remain. The sage, Yajñavalkya, said in the oldest Upanishad that it is only for the sake of realizing the true I, the Atman, that one gathers friends, wealth, experience or knowledge. One has life only for that. As Madame de Salzmann has so often said, "Without a contact with the real I, your life has no meaning. Without that relationship, you are nothing."

❖ ❖ ❖

Yesterday evening in the group meeting, Madame de Salzmann was very strong. I am repeatedly struck by how remarkable she is. I do not know why, but I felt sad to think that Krishnamurti never knew her. I suppose it is because Krishnamurti has been important to me and I wish he could have known Madame de Salzmann. Each of them has permitted me a very warm relationship, but quite differently. With him—vulnerable, like a wounded doe, and delicately aristocratic, like a solitary swan—I have often argued and occasionally joked, usually privately and sometimes in public forums. But with her—a fiery combination of a strong force and a penetrating insight—I rarely have even an inner argument. If I understand what she was saying, everything in me agrees.

I asked a question in English in order to be sure that I asked it correctly. I wanted to know about the fear of losing what I know and of being other than what I am, in other words, a fear of transformation.

I have such a fear, and it is perhaps my strongest fear. Sometimes when I push against it at the threshold, I have a sensation of fainting. But Madame de Salzmann did not let me finish the question. She spoke in English for a long time and said I was not open and my body was constricted. "One must be without any tension whatsoever. Then the finer energy comes by itself, automatically."

After a few minutes, she looked at me and said that now my body was much more open. She spoke very strongly, and at length, about the requirement of having an open and relaxed body, about the decision to work and the need for an inner commitment, about the necessity of the right posture, of punishing the body if necessary, and of conscious labour and intentional suffering. She said, "Now is a very special moment for the Work. Many things are now possible. It is very necessary to know how to work. On what? With what? Why? Absolutely clearly."

Paris, May 1985.

The Level Always Changes

How quickly one forgets—I forget—everything! I forget that I will die; that I did wish to pay for my existence, that I had understood how to work. So much time and energy are wasted in reaction and negativity. It is incredible! Imagination is verily the enemy; I need to struggle against it ceaselessly.

In the presence of Madame de Salzmann, it all seems so clear: what the work is and how I must struggle with myself, and why. But away from her, confusion and doubt return and I forget.

❖ ❖ ❖

Madame de Salzmann was coughing in a meeting, rather uncharacteristically. Nobody made any comment about it. But, quite unasked, she said, "It is not tension. It is the Spring." I was sure that she was reading our minds and could see that one of us had wondered about her being tense.

There are many instances in the Gospels when Christ responds to unarticulated questions and doubts of the disciples. I have been convinced for many years now that it is quite foolish and futile to try to hide anything from the teachers. If they are not sensitive enough to sense what is going on behind the masks of the pupils, they cannot in any case help. The important thing is to be naked in front of them, to allow oneself to be seen. That way they can help quickly and at the right place and time. It is quite ridiculous to go to a doctor because something is wrong with one, and then to try to cover up the symptoms so that the doctor does not find out precisely what the problem is.

❖ ❖ ❖

My wife and I were invited to a party at the de Salzmann's last evening. We had been in Paris for a couple of weeks and yesterday was our last evening there. I had arranged to take my wife out to a restaurant for a romantic evening on her birthday, before I had to leave for Montreal to give a lecture, and before her return to our home in Halifax. When Michel invited us I could hardly refuse even though it interfered with my well-laid plans for a grand evening in Paris.

At the party there were three or four generations of de Salzmanns and a few other people. The assembly reminded me of the gathering of a joint family in India, directed and guarded by the grand matriarch of the tribe. Michel played the role of the host, but most of the guests gathered around Madame de Salzmann. Before we arrived, Madame de Salzmann, Alain Kremski and some others had been working on the Gurdjieff/de Hartmann music which was to be published. Alain had just returned from having given concerts of the Gurdjieff/de Hartmann music in many countries, including Sri Lanka, Japan, China, Korea and Pakistan. There was a festive air in the room and the atmosphere was familial and gay.

Speaking about the master and pupils, Michel made a very interesting comment. He said, "There is no choice. One is, each one is, a master. The quality of the master is shown by the pupils. It is the pupils who make the master."

Later in the evening, one of the toasts he proposed was very metaphysical. Madame de Salzmann said that she did not understand what he had said, and she refused to drink the toast.

Michel has a very difficult role. "I always pay," he had said to me on one occasion. It has to be true: those who feel responsible are obliged to work; they must pay.

I went and sat near Madame de Salzmann. At one point during the evening, she said to me, "The Work has made much progress at many places. But it is necessary to raise the level still higher; otherwise it will fall and will get mixed up with other things. . . The level always changes. It must become either higher or lower, it cannot remain the same."

Paris, May 1985.

It Is Important
to Go towards Life

As I was traveling to New York I decided that I would not call upon Madame de Salzmann. I knew she was very busy and I did not wish to bother her. Besides, I did not really have anything to ask and I was convinced that I had not worked enough to deserve a meeting with her. When I arrived in New York, Mrs. Welch said that I must call Madame de Salzmann. "I have told her you are here. You must see her. She wishes to see you. She will actually be offended if you don't call." I was completely surprised, even shocked. I do not seem to be clear about the difference between consideration and considering and I am constantly mistaking one for the other. When I called the place where Madame de Salzmann was staying, she answered the phone herself and recognized me immediately. Right away she said, "Ah yes, perhaps you wish to see me?" What could I say? Of course! She said, "I can see you in a week." I said I was leaving New York before that. "Then, come tomorrow, at four."

❖ ❖ ❖

Madame de Salzmann has been working on a film of the Movements for several years. She wishes it to be a record of the quality of attention possible n the work of the Movements. It is stunning, particularly the men's Movements. The stage setting is especially remarkable. There are no walls and it seems as if space is crystallized on the top of the mountain where the Movements are taking place.

After the showing of the film, there was a group meeting. Mrs. Welch asked if someone would volunteer to take notes of the discussion about the Movements film. I offered and it was useful. I thought it could be a small payment for the privilege of seeing the film. It was only later that I realized the value of making an effort in approaching the meaning of the film. Can anything be understood without paying for it in some way?

❖ ❖ ❖

Here I am, having just spent forty-five minutes with Madame de Salzmann and having been coated by her presence. Immediately she asked, "How do you work? What do you sense?"

I told her about what I had tried, and described the movement of energy, and the effect on breathing, and other details. This is the first time I have heard and seen her really pleased with what I described. She said, "I see you have worked well, and hard, for a long time." Then she suggested that I work alone and also with others, teaching them, calling them to work. I said that somewhere deep down I feel that I do not really know, directly and substantially, and that I fear merely philosophizing. She said, "Of course one does not stay in touch with the higher energy very long. But one is helped by working with others."

Madame de Salzmann said that she is going to make another film. And she is nearly ninety-seven! She is not wholly satisfied with the new film on Movements, but she agreed that the men's Movements showed a fine and strong quality. Apropos the emphasis on the Movements, I asked her about those of us, like myself, who are not naturally gifted in the Movements. "Often the Movements are presented as the heart of the Work. What about those of us who are not good at the Movements?" She said, "That depends on how the Movements are brought. You can move very well, if you are taught properly."

I asked her about China, where I was planning to go for a few months. She said she does not know anyone there. "Perhaps you will tell me." Later she remarked, perhaps with my earlier question about China in mind, that there is something in the Work which is not easy to find elsewhere. She spoke about those who retire from the world and work by themselve alone. "It is important to go towards life, to maintain connection, and to call others to work."

Madame de Salzmann used an interesting expression in saying, "Some groups have sat down and people are stuck at some place, and nobody knows how to help them." A little later, she said, "You need to continue working. Strengthen your attention. It comes and goes, but stay in front of it." Then she led me through an exercise which she said I must practice twice a day. "In between come back to a sense of yourself—how you move, and walk."

She asked when she would see me again. "Can you come back to New York when I return, after a few days for three weeks or so?"

I said I would if she would let me know when. She insisted on having my address and phone number so that she could let me know.

I said that in any case I would likely come to Paris in May. "Good! Write or telephone before coming to find out if it is a good time. I think it will be."

As I was leaving, she came to the elevator door—as usual, with extreme courtesy, as if I had done her a favour by coming to see her—and said after a moment, "Now since I see how you work, it will be very good to work together. Can you write or telephone? Have you given your address also?"

What a remarkable lady! And here I did not want to bother her! I seem to be a completely unwilling and inactive student who does not even realize that he needs food, and certainly does not open his mouth to eat, but has to be force fed. I remember hearing several times from my father the moral from a story in the *Panchatantra* that "in a sleeping lion's mouth the deer do not enter." I wonder if it is really true. It seems to me that if a teacher takes interest in a student then she gives him food even if he has forgotten about it, as a mother might call a child from his playing to come and eat. A teacher-student relationship is not only about ideas. It is more a sharing of a subtle substance as among members of an extended spiritual family. An old Daoist proverb says it well: "One who is a teacher for a day is like a parent for life." I felt as if somehow by slow degrees I had become a member of Madame de Salzmann's spiritual family. This sort of thing is often spoken of in the Indian tradition: a real guru is like a parent who is related with the disciple through many incarnations. It is said that the physical birth takes place in the womb of the mother, but the spiritual birth in the womb of the heart of the guru.

I cannot not come to see her. She had told me quite sternly a few years earlier, "I have the freedom to say 'no'. You must call!"

New York, December 1985.

One Must Have an Action
in the World

It seems like a ritual I repeat. I am off to New York again, in the hope of spending a little time with Madame de Salzmann. I do not know what it is that I wish for, yet I am like a bee who is unable to stay away from nectar. Does a bee know what it wishes? Or does it follow a deep, subconscious instinct?

Madame de Salzmann had asked me to come back to New York and I could hardly stay away. It seems like the right time to be in New York. The Foundation is closed and Madame de Salzmann is here for the next two weeks without too many group meetings or other engagements. I understand she is concentrating on working with the senior people in the Work. However, she has said that I could come and see her. But what do I need to ask her? More instruction in meditation? Is she going to teach me something about the Movements, as she promised when I last met her three weeks ago? I have not been exactly rigorous in carrying out the tasks she gave me last time. Although it is true that I have been sick and very busy, this is a mere excuse. She has often said, quoting Gurdjieff, "Very good is not enough."

I seem to be under some sort of fate or destiny. This appears to be so with respect to other things in my life as well. So much of my life seems to be out of my hands, as if it is somehow inevitably and impersonally guided by some guardian angels. Maybe this is the way it is for everyone: we all seem to be pawns in the play of very large forces.

It certainly always seems like a good idea to come back again and again to what my need is. Do I in fact see that I am asleep and mechanical? Do I see that I am wasting my life, my potential? Am I aware that I have a calling, a destiny? How do I find out what it is and how do I respond to it? Here I am, at a stage of my life when I should be—and perhaps I am in fact—free of many laws of bondage. Now, I have access to a sufficient amount of time, money and energy, and the hold of the ego is also loosening a little. It does seem that I am at the threshold of a new phase in my life. Am I basically going to squander this opportunity and continue adding to my ego and hoarding what I have? Or am I going to be able to undergo a new birth? The central thing is to do what needs to be done, without fear and without self-importance.

❖ ❖ ❖

I had a very nourishing meeting with Madame de Salzmann. I gave her a copy of my article, "In the Beginning is the Dance of Love," which I had been invited to present at the meetings of the Royal Society of Canada in Montreal. She has often emphasized the importance of going towards life, but I have a great resistance about going to academic meetings. I told her about this and said that I am particularly distressed at the gatherings of scholars of religion. I do not imagine that religion scholars are any worse than others, but I expect something different from them. I believe that they would wish to practice a vulnerability to the Spirit, but what I find is that for most of the scholars the study of religion is a career. I keep wondering what the point of scholarship or knowledge is. I seem to have a very traditional perspective: I wish knowledge to lead to salvation and freedom.

Madame de Salzmann said, "It is important to realize that all religions lose contact with their real meaning as time passes. The same thing can happen with the Work if one is not careful. Sometimes one particular activity or idea is emphasized because it is needed; then one can make it into the whole thing and lose the real meaning behind it."

Madame de Salzmann spoke, as she often has, of making a connection with the energy (or force) which comes from the higher part of the mind, above the head. "Two things are necessary. For an hour or so, work very hard to be open to this energy. The body must be completely relaxed. I can sit like this (she demonstrated leaning against the couch) and still be open, because I have worked all my life. Otherwise, one needs to sit straight like this (she again demonstrated). Work like this two or even three times a day, each time for an hour or so. In between, try to maintain a sensation of the body.

"After working hard, then do simple things, without losing this presence, this contact with higher energy.

"Even when one is able to be open to this energy and experience it strongly, it does not stay long. The attention needs a movement to follow, as of breath or of sensation down the spine, as in some of the exercises. Otherwise, one cannot remain open. When the energies of the lower mind and of the body are together, then a new energy arises which can be open to the higher energy.

"You need to be more *exigeant* with yourself. Ask the body to cooperate; otherwise, punish it. Don't eat; or eat less. The body won't listen to ideas, but it will listen to direct commands like this. The body is very important, but it must obey.

"One cannot be without action; right action is needed in the world. Therefore, one needs to be simultaneously aware of both the higher and the lower currents of energy. The religious people often just want to sit and be open to higher energy.

"Every day work with one or two other people, or more. That will be very good for you. Work with them in a way that you don't hinder their work, but help them.

"It is all between your ego and your self. The second body needs to be substantially felt throughout the body."

New York, December 1985.

You Need to Develop Attention

Madame de Salzmann is wholly present when she speaks of the work. She does not only speak of it, she illustrates it. In a general discussion meeting today, she listened for a while, probably got a little impatient with the generally low level, and brought the meeting to heel with her usual, but ever fresh, reminder of the necessity of the connection between the mind and the body. She also spoke about the three forces—mind, body and feeling—needing to come together for a new life, or energy, to arise.

I have heard this so often, and it makes such clear sense in her presence. I even experience it occasionally. But, later, doubts come, as if I have a different mind, or some light is not there. Then confusion, or in any case a lack of connection, prevails. I mentioned all this to her when I saw her by myself in her office. She listened patiently and gave the advice I have often received: to keep practising and to stay in front.

More specifically, she said again to work two or three times a day, for twenty minutes or so each time, to make the connection between the mind and the body so that a higher part of the mind will open. "When the connection is not there, say, 'Love, have mercy.' Higher energy, which comes from the higher part of the mind, is Love." She said "Love" as if "Lord." I listened carefully. Twice again, she repeated it, and again I heard "Love." I was not expecting it, and was surprised. Love, have mercy.

Then she said, "You work two or three times a day, and then write to me telling me whether the higher part of your mind is open or not."

❖ ❖ ❖

It does not really matter what question one asks. Madame de Salzmann returns very quickly to the themes of the body and the mind not being connected, of attention not being very strong, of the higher energy from above the head with which one needs to be related, and of the need to stay in front of the lack of connection. What she sees is the state a person is in, and she begins from there. Very soon, of course, she wishes the person to attend to the necessary practice for connecting with the real.

She told me, "The most important exercise is to have the body as relaxed as possible in every situation. During quiet work, there should be no tension. That will allow the relationship with higher energy. You cannot do it, but be open to it. If there is no relationship, stay in front of the lack. When doing anything else, keep a sensation of the body. If you work like this then we can speak again."

After a little while, she said, "I can see you tomorrow." I was surprised, for I had not even asked to see her again so soon. She suggested eleven o'clock and made a note in her diary without asking my name.

I had asked about insincerity with oneself. I see the need for a connection with the higher energy, but then my behavior does not really show that I am interested in this. How can I take myself seriously? I do not really seem to be interested in working. Madame de Salzmann said that what is needed is the development of attention.

Later, I asked her a somewhat theoretical question: "I see how greedy I am: for information, for recognition, for money. But it is so absurd and stupid, for I have enough. Why am I greedy?"

She said, "That is how one is brought up. Everyone is like that. But one has a body for another purpose. The body is not only yours."

I keep wondering about the statement of Madame de Salzmann that "your body is not only yours." This statement is an invitation to let something higher occupy and use my body. Ideally, the highest God could inhabit my body. Only then could I be a microcosmos truly mirroring the macrocosmos. In a geometrical inversion which the symbols sometimes suggest, the highest in which I and the world are contained becomes the deepest within me. My body thus becomes the meeting place of the ray of creation outside and the ray of creation inside. If my body—or mind, energy, talents, money—is only mine, it cannot serve anything higher than myself. What do I serve? One cannot be true to oneself and refuse to respond to what calls, but from the level of the ordinary body–mind one cannot precisely know the goal, nor perhaps even the way. Only a deep, subconscious, inner instinct for what is real can guide us. I wonder if that is what is meant by the 'soul' or the 'particle of Divinity' in us. Why does it need a body? I need to understand directly what Madame de Salzmann said: "One has a body for another purpose."

New York, April–November 1986; London, January 1987.

Between the Ego and the Self

What is most important is the connection with higher energy. And when one is not related, one must stay in front of the lack of connection. Stay in front of whatever is taking place: stay in front of your connection or the lack of it. Stay in front.

❖

Without a contact with the real I, your life has no meaning. Without that relationship, you are nothing.

❖

One must be without any tension whatsoever. Then the finer energy comes by itself, automatically.

❖

Now is a very special moment for the Work. Many things are now possible. It is very necessary to know how to work. On what? With what? Why? Absolutely clearly.

❖

The level always changes. It must become either higher or lower, it cannot remain the same.

❖

It is important to realize that all religions lose contact with their real meaning as time passes. The same thing can happen with the Work if one is not careful. Sometimes one particular activity or idea is emphasized because it is needed; then one can make it into the whole thing and lose the real meaning behind it.

❖

The attention needs a movement to follow, as of breath or of sensation down the spine, as in some of the exercises. Otherwise, one cannot remain open. When the energies of the lower mind and of the body are together, then a new energy arises which can be open to the higher energy.

❖

You need to be more exigeant with yourself. Ask the body to cooperate; otherwise, punish it. Don't eat; or eat less. The body won't listen to ideas, but it will listen to direct commands like this. The body is very important, but it must obey.

❖

One cannot be without action; right action is needed in the world. Therefore, one needs to be simultaneously aware of both the higher and the lower currents of energy.

❖

It is all between your ego and your self. The second body needs to be substantially felt throughout the body.

❖

One has a body for another purpose. The body is not only yours.

What Do You Really Wish?

Madame de Salzmann met with some Canadians in New York. She had an extraordinary presence. As she often has, she emphasized the importance of the right posture so that there is no tension at all. Then the energy from the higher part of the mind can enter into the body.

Madame de Salzmann looked at those in the first row and commented on the internal states of various people. To me she said, "You can be very open and have a deep connection. But be careful about the relationship with the body.

I understood that to mean that I can contact the higher energy, but that I should be careful not to lose contact with the body. Perhaps I have a mystical tendency to fly away and leave the ground. To fly away from the Earth is certainly a deep inclination of the Indian spiritual traditions and I could hardly have escaped it.

❖ ❖ ❖

During the work day at the Foundation, the usual play of forces, wishing to be present as well as giving in to passivity, was evident, inside myself and also in others. Somewhat unexpectedly, it was mentioned that Madame de Salzmann was going to come at 3:30 p.m. The news galvanized everybody. She came and worked with the energy in the group like a maestro conducting an orchestra. She even moves her hands like that! She has one central thing to say, or to demonstrate. It does not matter what anybody asks or says, Madame de Salzmann quickly returns to speak of the energy that comes from the higher part of the mind and which can come into the body when there is no tension anywhere.

Yesterday as well as today, the two groups in which I participated worked very well in the presence of Madame de Salzmann. The two groups were very different from each other, but the people in both of them have been quite well prepared in attitude and practice. It takes so long to understand anything subtle; I can well appreciate why Madame de Salzmann said that it is important to live long.

In the presence of Madame de Salzmann, all the other senior people, men and women, seem so small and frail. All of these people are impressive in their own ways, but they pale in her presence. I wonder if the Work will be in danger after her departure. To the extent the Work serves an objective need, other capable and wise people will certainly rise to the occasion after her death. If it does not serve something objective and higher, it does not matter whether it survives or not. But, it is important to remember that we need to inquire without fear and without vanity. Truth seeks us more than we seek her.

❖ ❖ ❖

I took a copy of my article on Krishnamurti, "The Mill and the Millpond," to give to Madame de Salzmann. She was sitting there reading a book by Krishnamurti in French. She started reading my article then and there. Knowing that my time was short I had to say to her a couple of times that I was going to leave the article with her. Finally, she put it down and said she would read it later.

Towards the end of his life I had had a long conversation with Krishnamurti about death. Before going to see Madame de Salzmann I had thought it would be a good idea if I asked her also some questions about death. I felt the importance of understanding something about death but I was not clear what my question was, so I did not raise anything with her about this.

I asked her about the relationship of the higher energy with breathing, the question I had tried to ask in the group meeting earlier.

WHAT DO YOU REALLY WISH?   173

She said, essentially, that the body is shocked by the coming of the higher energy and it acts in all sorts of ways. I am quite certain that by the "body" she means something like *sharira* in the *Bhagavad Gita* or "flesh" in the *Gospel According to St. John*. It includes thinking and emotions at the level of the planetary body. When the ordinary mind reasserts itself and begins to comment on this or that or about higher energy, she would say that it is the automaton of the body. The higher energy is not of the body, but can be in the body. The 'body' is the lower (personal, egocentric) being. She used to say "the energy of the mind" or "the energy which comes from above the mind." Now she says more that this "energy comes from the higher part of the mind." But, in any case, it is not personal or egoistic.

I also described to her that sometimes for a week or so it is easier to connect with higher energy, and sometimes for days or weeks it is much harder. She said, "That is quite normal. Our attention is not developed enough to sustain it."

I said that I am interested in the relationship of this energy with sex. Sometimes, during the days when I am more able to connect with the higher energy, I am also more interested in sex. She said, "This energy touches every part of the body, including sex. Then one feels the sexual impulse and wants to express it. But one does not always have to have the usual action."

I reported to her that I see that I am very vain and arrogant, and that I see more and more how much energy and how many opportunities of learning are wasted because of my vanity. I see that to be vain is stupid; nothing is gained by that. She said, "Yes, you are vain, but not always. Sometimes you are open."

I have often noticed that Madame de Salzmann is not very interested in criticism or elaboration of manifestations. She is much more interested in the ability to see the manifestations. I remember reading in *Mount Analogue* about the necessity of "submitting the visible to the power to see." Seeing belongs to a world higher than that of manifestation, and it is the higher world, or the higher energy, to which she constantly returns. She herself presents such an excellent example of someone in touch with higher energy.

Madame de Salzmann asked me to speak about my work, and to describe to her the moment in the work for which I strive and which is the most important. I told her that it is a vibration, or a sensation, or presence which gives me a feeling of being connected with something higher. It is spread throughout the torso, but I experience it more quite low down. I literally have a sense of more space, as if I am expanded inside. She seemed very interested, and smiled.

Madame de Salzmann said, "Nothing lasts long. One has to begin again and again. There are these two forces, from above and from below. One comes from above the head, the other from the body. One needs the body and it is important, but it must not take over. It has no meaning by itself. It exists for something else."

I remembered that she had said, "Your body is not only yours." Clearly, it must serve something higher, otherwise, it has no meaning. She asked me to work a few times a day in the way she was now indicating, with no tensions anywhere, sitting attentively, open to the higher energy, and then to report to her. She entered an appointment in her notebook for me two days later, without even asking me whether I would still be in New York. Now I have to stay.

Madame de Salzmann said, "You should work with others. You will see that gradually your attention will develop so that you can stay longer in touch with higher energy."

Later, Madame de Salzmann asked me, "What do you really wish?"

I said, "Sometimes, at my deepest, I wish to serve something real and true. But sadly, so often I just wish to feel special and important. I more feel the need and wish to know the truth when I realize that younger people ask me something or depend on me to help them." It was all simple and true, and she seemed happy.

She said, "You should work with others. It is necessary. It will help you."

New York, December 1987.

Always Try Something

Madame de Salzmann will be ninety-nine in about a month. She was at a senior group meeting at five-thirty, and at a reading at six-thirty. Then she came to the eight-thirty meeting, strongly maintaining attention and inspiring everyone for an hour. She finally stopped because others must have been tired and could not take it any more. She herself certainly could have continued. I have often wondered if there is something in us which never tires. This is simply a subset of an assertion of all religions that there is something in us which never dies. Watching her, one can easily be convinced of miracles.

What Madame de Salzmann says is familiar enough, at one level. It is her repeated demonstration of the fact of it, as by a master artist, which is striking. This is what makes her words ever fresh. She is certainly in touch with a higher energy. She says that our connection with higher energy needs to develop more; it is for this that one works and lives.

I said, "It must be the case that I do not really see or feel the need for working. Otherwise, why don't I work? I am not serious enough. I do not wish to pay for the connection with higher energy."

I do not know whether she heard what I said. She did not seem to accept that I am not at all serious. "Do you believe that?" she asked.

When I am in her presence, I do feel some sort of a connection and need for working. Soon afterwards I forget about working. How can I regard myself as serious? Sometimes I feel that I have never worked. I seem to be hounded by God, and I see that God and the Devil are fighting with each other in the arena of my soul, but I have nothing to do with it. I do not remember very often what I really wish; and I spend most of my time and energy in self-importance, seeking pleasures and acquisitions. I can hardly be called a warrior of the Spirit. How can I take myself seriously? I cannot say that I really see that there is a sacred purpose to my existence, that I am on the planet for a reason, or that anything depends on me. I believe this because of the emphasis placed on it by Madame de Salzmann, and in her presence it makes sense to me. But I do not know this directly and permanently. In that sense, it is not a fact for me.

❖ ❖ ❖

I have seen Madame de Salzmann individually or in a group every day for the past five days. The frequency of the meetings with her reminded me of the contacts I had with her in Paris several years ago. She is very strong indeed; when she speaks about inner work, she is wholly vibrant and alive.

"There are three forces—of the body, mind and feeling. Unless these are together, equally developed and harmonized, a steady connection cannot be made with a higher force. Everything in the Work is a preparation for that connection. That is the aim of the Work. The higher energy wishes to but cannot come down to the level of the body unless one works. Only by working you can fulfill your purpose and participate in the life of the cosmos. This is what can give meaning and significance to your life. Otherwise, you exist only for yourself, egoistically, and there is no meaning to your life.

"You must always be conscience.* Even if a little, always try something. Do not be in reaction. When you speak, walk or do anything, keep a little sensation. This area [pointing to the belly] is especially important. It is important to have no tension there."

Later, during the meditation sitting, Madame de Salzmann said, "Lord, have mercy. Lord is the higher energy. Say it to yourself three or four times and open to the higher energy."

❖ ❖ ❖

I had lunch with the Welches. Mrs. Welch said she is happy about my persistence which enables me to see Madame de Salzmann so often. I told her that it has nothing to do with my persistence at all. I do not even ask for these meetings, but before I leave Madame de Salzmann asks something like, 'When do I see you next?' or 'Perhaps you can come tomorrow?' What can I say? I seem to be like a man with a peculiar kind of disease: he feels no hunger and does not look for food; only when he is force fed he realizes that he needs the food and that he will die without it. I do not understand what is going on. I am given so much, but I live completely selfishly. Unless the work gets into me in spite of myself, I shall die wholly wrapped up in the shell of my own self-occupation and I shall perish into perdition. Lord, have mercy.

Mrs. Welch asked me what was interesting me these days in my work in the groups. I told her that I have been coming back to a remark of Madame de Salzmann's from several years back, which I now understand as if for the first time: "The Lord, the *Seigneur*, is there but he needs my body to come. The body is not ready. It needs to be prepared. If the mind and the body are connected then the higher energy, which is what religions call *Seigneur*, will appear."

New York, December 1987.

---

*She meant to say 'conscious.' The French is in fact closer to the mark: there can be no higher consciousness without higher conscience.

Your Work Is Necessary

Why am I in New York again? And so soon after having been here? I came to be in the presence of Madame de Salzmann. She continues to amaze me, enthrall me and beckon me. In her presence there is always a clearer internal order. I do not have any specific questions or directions to ask of her, but perhaps I can be in her atmosphere for a little while, imbibing a little higher energy.

The 'January 13th' celebration at the Foundation was a grand affair, with elaborate Middle-Eastern decor and food, served very well to more than two hundred people. What an enormous amount of work goes into arranging an evening like that! Also, how necessary it is to have occasions and rituals like these. These occasions help create a sacred calendar for people in the Work so that they can participate in the rhythms of time more intentionally and sacramentally.

The presence of Madame de Salzmann makes any occasion special. She was in fine form, full of energy, speaking strongly and inviting questions, moving to music as in a dance. She spoke about the necessity of working; otherwise, "the Earth will fall." I do not really understand what she means by this, even though something in me feels its rightness. Later, I asked a senior person in the Work what sense he made of it. He said he did not know, and that as far as he was concerned such statements are for the apostles or the abbots. "If His Endlessness is depending on me, He has poor management!"

There was a reading from one of Madame de Salzmann's talks in Paris in 1979. It was strong and succinct. "Everyone is imprisoned in their physical postures and attitudes, and the consequent emotional and mental postures. It is necessary to find a way of being which frees one from this limitation. It is necessary to find a connection with higher energy."

Madame de Salzmann very much emphasized the need to have an action, an activity, in life, in order to express and manifest higher energy. She also stressed the necessity of a struggle inside so that the body and the feeling would be engaged; only then a transformation can take place. "Ideas are necessary, otherwise one is trapped by impressions, but they are not sufficient by themselves. One must have an action."

She also spoke about a whole new kind and level of relationship that can come about when one is in touch with higher energy. I remembered that once in Paris, speaking about a similar theme, she had suddenly said, as if experiencing a different taste of a connection with a superior energy, *"C'est fantastique!"*

There were many very fine and moving moments in the evening. For me, the most touching one was when Madame de Salzmann, in one of her periodic attempts to raise the energy of the assembled group, invited people to speak, to ask questions and to work. There was a lack of quality and vitality in the response. She said with much feeling, "Please work and ask questions. I am nearly a hundred. I wish my life to be useful before I die."

I was touched to the core. She needs our work to give meaning to her life. If I do not work and lessen her burden, how could I imagine carrying out the aim suggested by Gurdjieff of lessening the sorrow of His Endlessness?

❖ ❖ ❖

I have just had a meeting with Madame de Salzmann which deeply nourished me. As I arrived I asked Madame de Salzmann how she felt. She said she was well and that there were a lot of things to do. I remarked that she looked very well and vigorous, and I asked what the secret of her energy was. She said, "I used to ask the same question of Mr.

Gurdjieff. Sometimes I would remind him to rest and not to work so hard, and he would say that it was necessary. But, you see, then he went away." She seemed to mean that he died too soon, as if prematurely. In that one remark she conveyed the immensity of the work remaining to be done, some left unfinished after Gurdjieff's early death.

Madame de Salzmann asked me what question I wished to raise. I said primarily I just wished to be in her presence. That was the most important thing, although I did have some questions.

I asked Madame de Salzmann how to understand that the Earth will fall if we do not work. She said, "It is necessary to face the idea that the Earth will fall if we do not work. This will help your work and help you understand that your work is necessary."

I said that I have some feeling for this idea, and a little sense of it, but that I do not really understand it. I do think that if I could see that somehow my work is necessary for the Earth, or for a larger purpose, then I would feel less self-centered, and more related with the need for working. It occurred to me that this was a cosmological way of saying that there is a purpose to my existence, and that I need to fulfill it. Otherwise, a lower cosmological function—so stylishly expressed by Gurdjieff as being 'food for the Moon'—is all that my life would satisfy. Either I live mechanically and feed the Moon, or I work to live a little more consciously and help the Earth.

Madame de Salzmann repeatedly asked, "How do you work? What do you feel? What questions do you have?"

I told her about the movement of energy in my body and where I experienced it. I also said that sometimes I sense an energy from above my head, and sometimes from between the eyes. She said that the latter is not so high; the former can be related with a very high energy.

I wanted to check with her again, as I had done many years earlier, about the rightness of some specific breathing exercises, especially since Gurdjieff seems to have been so much against them. I said that I found these breathing exercises very helpful in quieting the mind and in making a connection with the body. Since I wanted to be sure, I said I would show her what I do and how I sit. So I took off my shoes and sat in the lotus position on the floor in front of her and did the breathing exercise. I did it only once in order to show her. She asked me where the air comes from which I breathe. I tried to describe to her where I sense it in the body, mostly in the throat and down in the belly. She said it is important to be aware of the air just as it enters the nostrils and how it expands in the head. "The whole head opens and participates in breathing. You will see which part specifically makes connection with higher energy."

Madame de Salzmann asked many detailed questions about the currents I sense when working, and the movement of the energy inside. She also spoke about "the need to work and move in life after working quietly and trying to keep some connection. Not to speak s-l-o-w-l-y, but to find a way by which the connection can be maintained while working at a normal tempo. Try with different people. Especially in the beginning, it is easier with some people than with others. It is easier with people in the Work.

"If you work like this, tomorrow maybe you come and show me for a few minutes."

Meanwhile, I was sitting cross-legged in front of her, with a shaft of sunlight falling on me, and also her penetrating gaze. She again asked me to come and show her my work before I left for Canada. I was hesitating a bit in agreeing to come to see her again because I did not want to annoy the various guardians who have a very difficult job regulating the flow of people who wish to meet her. But I also wished to see her again. I asked her to enter a time for me in her notebook for Sunday. But she insisted that I should see her for a few minutes tomorrow (Saturday); then I can come again on Sunday.

Madame de Salzmann asked, "When do you come next to New York?"

I said, "The end of February, but by that time you might be gone back to Paris."

She said that she did not yet know when she would leave. "In any case, you can call me any time and I shall see you."

What a generous teacher she is! A master never spares herself, even when the pupil is lazy and does not know what to ask for.

❖ ❖ ❖

When I reached the place where I was staying I made some notes. Before I could finish writing I had a strong urge to sit and meditate. During quiet work, I felt and understood what early Christians might have meant by their prayer *Maranatha* (Lord Come). Someone is crying in the wilderness asking to make straight the path of the Lord. The higher energy is there, and could hardly be other than the Christ, but there is no clear path in the body for this energy. One can work and with one's attention make a channel in the body for this energy. Then the Kingdom—which is in Heaven, above the head—can come down to the Earth, in the body, and His will can be done on Earth as it is done in Heaven. But we are tempted and we are not delivered from evil. We remain in sin, and the Earth, at least our Earth in this body, falls down and is not nourished by the Christ, the Bread from Heaven.

Indeed, Lord have mercy. *Maranatha!*

New York, January 1988.

The Energy that Comes from Above

My wife and I were invited to the de Salzmanns' for lunch. As I had hoped, we had a brief meeting with Madame de Salzmann. Michel came into the room, saw us engaged with her, and went out. She asked if we were supposed to do something else, or meet with Michel rather than with her, and that if that were the case she could do something else meanwhile. We assured her that we wanted to see her. She said, "Since we have some private moments we should speak about the work." This is the only thing that really interests her; everything else is secondary. In order to hear her better and to be a little closer, I sat on the floor; that way she could also have a clear look at me. I asked her a question, and she asked me what I felt was most lacking. I said, "Attention. Not only in quiet work, but generally in working on anything, even reading." She seemed to agree and talked about the necessity of strengthening attention.

I had once said to her that to me it always sounds a little odd when people refer to Gurdjieff as "Mr. Gurdjieff," especially those people who did not personally know him. As far as I am concerned, something is thereby diminished. After all, we do not call Plato, Mr. Plato or Dante, Mr. Dante. She had agreed with me, but said it was different for those who knew him. In any case, in general, I heard her refer to him as Mr. Gurdjieff, and occasionally in some context only as Gurdjieff. Now, to my surprise, in a quick succession twice she referred to him by his first name. She said when she worked with Georgivanovich she would sometimes ask him, when he was very tired, to rest, and take a break from working. He always said, "Ah, that is not possible." Of course, that is her own situation: she cannot stop working unless others take over the work she now does.

The lunch with Madame de Salzmann, Michel and Josée was very pleasant. Michel said, in a semi-jocular manner, that his mother was living so long because she had yet not finished what she came to do. After lunch we spoke with Michel in his office. Again, he mentioned his idea of a journal of the Work community or *Sangha*, as he referred to it. Perhaps I shall write about "Buddhi Yoga of Krishna and the Work" for that journal.

❖ ❖ ❖

In a group meeting with Madame de Salzmann I had such a strong impression of myself as not serious about the work. I often spare myself and make excuses. It was a look at myself from a relatively more objective conscience.

Yesterday evening in the meeting, Madame de Salzmann was in great form. In fact, I do not think I have ever seen her as strong, and for so long. The sheer length of time for which she was present in the meeting, two full hours, was striking. I was completely spent by the end of it, and my back was bothering me from my attempts to sit straight. And she, almost twice my age, sat there like a great monument. She had earlier had a meeting from six until seven. No doubt she saw someone in between, and came to our meeting at seven-thirty. While leaving our meeting nearly two hours later, she asked someone to see her alone. She is never tired, it seems. There can hardly be any question that she is connected with a great reservoir of energy which feeds and sustains her.

The group was particularly fractious and argumentative, but she did not react. Again and again she would start anew, from one angle or another, emphasizing the need for the right posture of the body, the need for a total lack of tension, the need for a relationship between the mind and the body, the need for sensation, the need for strong attention.

It is very interesting to see how she conducts a group, or rather the energy in the group. She often moves her hand, usually the right one, as if she is actually conducting an orchestra. Energies—or angels, I dare say—move up and down in response to her movements. She raises questions or speaks about the higher energies, always acting, never reacting.

Madame de Salzmann seems to see people's inner states clearly, where they are tense, and whether they are present or not. I said that something in me is not convinced that I am necessary in the vast universe, or that my work is required. That is one way, in any case, that I avoid working. She did not respond to my specific remark but spoke generally. To some extent it really does not matter what one says or asks. Madame de Salzmann seems to have only one single insistence: how to connect with the energy that comes from above and how to remain connected with it. She herself demonstrates this connection, and the attendant state of freedom, primarily from identification and reaction. This connection is the one thing needful to attempt. Everything else is secondary.

Every time Madame de Salzmann seemed about to bring the meeting to a close, someone in the group would ask a question or make a statement, and she would begin again, almost as if the meeting was just starting. This went on and on. One of the persons who was carrying on at length was invited by her to lead the others into quiet work. He tried for a few minutes and then she took over. After a little while she asked us to see how the energy was now lowered. It was true. She even led us through a simple movement of raising one arm, then another, without losing connection with the energy from above. All in all, she pulled out all the stops; it was a wholly stunning meeting. After all this, she seemed to have no need to be alone or to rest. She invited the man whom she had asked to lead the quiet work, and who had been particularly argumentative and difficult, to go with her to her room. What was she doing? Certainly pushing everybody to their limits.

In a way one could say that Madame de Salzmann is not saying anything new now, but she continually demonstrates what she is speaking about. She does not say anything novel; but she is always original, for she is related to the Origin and she speaks from the Source. Her very presence nourishes the soul. In front of her one can sense directly what she said in the meeting: "The energy that comes from above is the second body. It can be felt in the whole of the body."

Paris, April 1988.

The Need for Inner Freedom

During my short visit to Paris, I have been given as much as I could hope for, and more. Madame de Salzmann was so vibrant in the meeting last evening. She may have no idea which country or which group she is in, but when she talks about the work, she is related with another energy. She wanted people to speak about their work. At one point she directly asked me to speak. It was mostly the foreigners, an American couple and my wife and myself, who engaged with her in the meeting.

After the meeting, one of the French gentlemen actually thanked us for our presence. "*Votre présence a vivifié Madame de Salzmann. Vos questions et même votre langue sont plus direct que les nôtre. . .*" ("Your presence vivified Madame de Salzmann. Your questions and even your language are more direct than ours. . .") Perhaps he does not realize that we foreigners cannot express any subtle nuance in French; what we say has to be direct and elemental.

During the meeting I repeated my observation about the energy descending but not re-ascending. I come back to this quite often, for I sense something important in this. She said that to sense the energy descending is more important. As always, she stressed the necessity of working long and for several times a day, and of having the right posture, relaxation, strong attention, and other things. "The upper part of the head has to open."

Madame de Salzmann remarked about my 'yes' and no'. I know I am mixed. I need to see myself more and more clearly.

❖ ❖ ❖

A friend is dying of cancer. How obvious it is that one must come to terms with disease and death. That seems to have been the catalyst for the search of the Buddha. Any one of us, and completely suddenly, without warning, can lose our functions or our life at any time. How little one knows! Lord have mercy.

Madame de Salzmann had a tumor removed on Saturday and she was out for a walk on Tuesday, and at the meditation sitting on Wednesday. She is quite amazing.

I have been wondering about the need for sacrifice and an internal purity. In meditation, how can one let go of what is not necessary: tensions, reactions, thinking. If sin is what is unnecessary—as Ouspensky quotes Gurdjieff saying—how can I be sinless and pure while sitting? Much of the secret seems to be in being active without doing anything. I recall Krishnamurti once saying: "Be wholly alert but do nothing."

I do not have any questions to ask. I am nourished by the vibration of the Work. I need to be here, in the Work Sangha, breathing the same air as the other fellow searchers. It is a food. There is no question about it; one just needs to eat. Nothing new needs to be known. It is much the same food: one needs to eat again and again. It is the same act; but one needs to make love again and again. But the same act, or the same eating of food, refreshes, if one is hungry for it and has need of it. Krishna is always celibate. Mary is perpetually virgin. Madame de Salzmann says the same thing, but she is ever fresh.

❖ ❖ ❖

Going to sleep last night, I was seized by fear. I was afraid of breathing out and felt I would not be able to breathe in again. I remembered experiencing the same fear a year ago in Madras. It is a fear of death and of dying, and of having to face the pointlessness of my existence. I thought of Madame de Salzmann and her teaching about the need of strength of attention. She had said that it was important to live long because there is much that needs to be understood and to be accomplished. She had also said that the energies of different levels do not die at the same time, for they have different durations. I wondered what will survive in me? Am I only a mechanism, a collection of bones, nerves and electrical stimuli? Is there nothing else?

My conscience was not at ease about the lack of intensity in my work for a connection with another quality of being. That seems to be the root of the fear of non-being. I saw that one needs to truly see and understand that there are higher energies. They are the ones which brought me here, to this cosmic celebration. I did not make myself. I understood the need for prayer, faith and self-surrender. It is important to realize the fact of the presence of the higher, otherwise, one is wholly on one's own ego resources, and one is rightly afraid. I remembered Madame de Salzmann telling me that I do not love my Self enough, but I love myself too much.

❖ ❖ ❖

It seems clear that the only way to engage Madame de Salzmann with the question one raises is to work innerly while speaking. In the group meetings, whenever I could manage, I tried to sit right in front of her. This seemed to me to be the only sensible thing to do.

In a group meeting, again and again, she emphasized the importance of the right posture and of bodily relaxation. She spoke a great deal about the need for inner freedom and the difficulty of coming to it. There was a remarkable exchange between her and several people. She would look at people's states and remark on whether they were connected or not. She said to me, "I see you have tried many things. You have a connection, but it needs to be stronger."

In response to one of her rhetorical questions to the whole group, "Is this how you work?" or "Is this how you wish to work?"

I said, "Yes, Madame!" in a way implying a request to work more intensely right now.

She said, "Not everyone present wishes to work like this. Some people are here for something else."

I wondered who was spoiling the occasion for serious work. It is clear how one person's resistance can spoil the opportunity of the whole group. She sees each person's wish and ability and responds to them accordingly, not sentimentally. How fortunate we are to have her in our midst!

❖ ❖ ❖

It seems increasingly clear that a transformation of the whole being— body, mind and soul—is needed. For that, meditation can be helpful, as can the Movements. But nothing alone will do.

I asked Michel de Salzmann about the problem of 'me, me, me' all the time, which is especially visible in quiet work, even when there is no specific object of ambition or assertion.

He said, "That is where the battle is needed. The me is an archaic organization, from childhood, and gives one security. And a great deal of work, even in the Work, is invested in that. One can be happy about that and have satisfaction. But as I, or buddhi, becomes clearer, then one is not oriented as much to the me in the body as to the I above. Then it shifts from 'I am happy' to 'The Lord is joyful.' Through me the energy has gone to make the Lord happy. That is the meaning of *Kyrie Eleison*. It does not mean 'Lord, have mercy'; it more means 'Lord, be joyful.' The body is the arena in which the forces of the world and those of I (Lord) battle."

Michel was very strong and clear in the meditation sitting. "Immediately, stop thinking. Not a time trip, but entering into now." Later, he emphasized listening to the resonance in oneself of 'I am', 'I wish to be', 'I can be', and entering into it. "The lower one goes down the central axis in oneself, the higher one can go."

Paris, April 1988; New York, June and December 1988.

Meaning and Significance of Life

Nothing lasts long. One has to begin again and again. There are these two forces, from above and from below. One comes from above the head, the other from the body. One needs the body and it is important, but it must not take over. It has no meaning by itself. It exists for something else.

❖

There are three forces—of the body, mind and feeling. Unless these are together, equally developed and harmonized, a steady connection cannot be made with a higher force. Everything in the Work is a preparation for that connection. That is the aim of the Work. The higher energy wishes to but cannot come down to the level of the body unless one works. Only by working you can fulfill your purpose and participate in the life of the cosmos. This is what can give meaning and significance to your life. Otherwise, you exist only for yourself, egoistically, and there is no meaning to your life.

❖

Even if a little, always try something. Do not be in reaction. When you speak, walk or do anything, keep a little sensation. This area [pointing to the belly] is especially important. It is important to have no tension there.

❖

Everyone is imprisoned in their physical postures and attitudes, and the consequent emotional and mental postures. It is necessary to find a way of being which frees one from this limitation. It is necessary to find a connection with higher energy.

❖

Ideas are necessary, otherwise one is trapped by impressions, but they are not sufficient by themselves. One must have an action.

❖

It is necessary to face the idea that the Earth will fall if we do not work. This will help your work and help you understand that your work is necessary.

❖

The energy that comes from above is the second body. It can be felt in the whole of the body.

❖

How Would You Invite God to Touch You?

I had written ahead to Madame de Salzmann before coming to New York, but I did not want to get too anxious about seeing her. I know she is very busy and that she is working with the senior people who take responsibility for so many people in various groups. However, I do not wish to be passive, so I made some effort to contact her, hoping that I could place myself near or in her gaze. But, then, it shall be as it should be. After all, the higher forces should be allowed to have some say in the matter. If I keep pushing, asking for this and that, everything that comes to me will be controlled from my level and therefore cannot be higher than myself.

It really is hard to accept the simple fact that from my usual level I do not know what I need and what is good for me. Even when I do know, which sometimes does happen in an attitude of vulnerability on my part, I do not have the force to actualize what I need. It is important to learn to wait, without expectation and manipulation, but with some aspiration and willingness. I remember in Paris, on occasions when I had not been able to get through to Madame de Salzmann, I would quietly wait at the Maison, trying to work as best I could. She would walk by and ask me to see her. Many a time, I was not even looking for her, for I had been given so much food that I did not feel hungry. I would just be sitting there, in the interval between my Movements classes and meetings, when Madame de Salzmann would walk by and ask me something like, "Why have you not called? I was looking for you. Come with me!"

I think it is my *karma* to be in her presence. I cannot alter it. Perhaps no one else can either. There were occasions, though, when I did not have the strength to have another meeting with her, or when out of some consideration for the organizational structure of the Work, I would not go with her. Whenever I said I had another meeting or a class to go to, she would never interfere with the form, but she would always insist that I come and see her as soon as I finished with my engagement. I could neither get to see her when she did not want to meet me; nor could I escape meeting with her when she wanted to see me.

This morning, I called the Foundation to find out if there was a message for me from Madame de Salzmann about my appointment with her. I thought there was something wrong with the number. When the phone was answered I identified myself before asking if there was any message for me. It was Madame de Salzmann's granddaughter on the phone. By mistake I had telephoned her house, where Madame de Salzmann was staying. In a few minutes I was able to speak with Michel de Salzmann, who had just arrived from Paris. He not only made an appointment for me to see his mother, but also to meet with him the next morning.

Is this all accidental? Surely there are forces which work behind the scenes, through our subconscious perhaps. How little one knows about what is really going on! It can hardly be that there is no meaning to *karma*, destiny and fate.

❖ ❖ ❖

I went to meet with Madame de Salzmann.

"You look well, Madame!"

"I feel fine. I am older than I look. Very soon I will be more than a hundred years old."

"You have defied the Merciless Heropass. I am only half your age."

"I do not feel old at all. When I see people who are twenty or thirty, I feel I can do everything they can. Of course, in some things I feel older. But time can also give something important. It was the same with Mr. Gurdjieff. He was old, but nobody felt a lack of energy in him."

"You will probably live twenty more years."

"I don't know. It is not important how long one lives, but whether one develops something which can give meaning to life. What do you wish in life? Why are you on the Earth?"

"As long as I can remember I have been interested in philosophical ideas. I have talked about Truth and God. But I don't know these solidly. They remain abstractions. I wish to have a knowledge which is solid. I wish to touch God."

"Or be touched by God!"

"Yes, I wish to be touched by God."

"If God were here close to you and He does not touch you, or at least you think He does not touch you, how would you invite Him to touch you? How would you open to Him?"

"What needs to be sacrificed? How to open? I often clearly understand the need to be open, to work. But I forget. Deep down, I don't see the need to work. How to remember?"

"Is your body necessary? Can you do without the body?"

"I don't know."

"You need to know, to know very well. At present you need your body. He allows you to make connections with other energies. You need to know your body well, and his automatism at many levels.

"Why do you work? I can see very well that you work, and often make connection. But it does not last. Nevertheless it is very good. You can go very far. But it depends on how you work. At present for you it is 'me, me, me'. Sometimes there is God also. Sometimes both God and me are there equally. But soon again it's 'me, me, me'. What is your relationship with the body? Why do you have a body?"

"The most persistent response, which is the truest for me, is that I wish to know myself, so that I can serve what needs to be served. But soon I forget this, and a generalized restlessness remains. I feel I am missing something, but I don't know what."

"What are you? Who are you?" she said strongly, her words and gaze hitting me like thunderbolts.

After some hesitation, I said quietly, "I am a seeker, a searcher of God."

"I can see very well you know how to work. But it needs to be stronger. Work like this for two or three days and come and see me again."

"I would very much like to, but I know there are many people who wish to come and see you."

"I don't see many people. I see only who I wish to see. It is important that I see you. It is not a question of many people. It is a play of forces." She spoke more and more strongly. "You work like this and telephone me. When you wish, I will be with you."

I had a strong feeling that she was not talking about being with me necessarily physically. I also had a sense of 'farewell' from her.

"You work like this for two or three days and come and see me. Or I shall telephone you. How old are you now?"

"Fifty."

"That is very good. You are young. You can go far."

When it was time for me to leave, Madame de Salzmann insisted on getting up from the couch and coming to the elevator to see me off. She stood there, holding the door open until I got into the elevator, and said, "Don't forget. Come and see me soon."

As I went into the street, and for a long time afterwards, her question kept ringing in my ears: "If God were here close to you and He does not touch you, or at least you think He does not touch you, how would you invite Him to touch you? How would you open to Him?"

New York, December 1988.

Why Don't You Work?

I met Dr. Dikran Dervichian in Paris during a day of work at the Maison. He was Armenian by origin and had spent some time in Egypt, where he had learnt Arabic. He was an admirer of the Muslim esoteric tradition which he had encountered in Egypt where, according to him, this tradition flourished very much in interaction with Coptic Christianity. We liked each other from the start, and even though he was much older than I was, we soon became essence friends. We met often, particularly when I visited Paris by myself, and we spoke at length about the Work.

When I first met Dikran, in 1980, he had just retired from *L'institut Pasteur* where he had been a biochemist of some note for a couple of decades. We often spoke about the underlying philosophy of the contemporary sciences, and we had agreed quite early in our conversations that science provides a very good intellectual discipline but that it does not nourish the soul. Especially now, as he was retired, Dikran wanted to spend most of his time reading and thinking about spiritual matters. We often spoke about the practice of spirituality, and especially as taught in the Work. He had been in the Work for about thirty years and regarded it to be the most important thing in his life.

We had very often said to each other that we were fortunate in having encountered the Work, and we imagined what our life would be if we had not met the Work. In one of our meetings, Dikran became very sad when the conversation came around to our congratulating ourselves for having the great fortune of meeting the Work. He told me of an incident that had happened the day before:

"I had gone to see Madame de Salzmann who rather likes me. I found myself saying to her what we have often spoken about, namely that I am so fortunate to be in the Work. I told her how and when I had met the Work, with whom I had worked and in what groups I had been and with whom I was working now. I was speaking at length, and telling her about my involvement in the Work for the last thirty years. Again I told her how grateful I was to her and to the Work, and that without the Work my life would have no meaning.

"Suddenly, she looked at me with a penetrating look which had both an enormous disappointment and hope in it. What she said has pierced me very deeply, and I cannot rest easy any more. She said, 'If you are so fortunate to find the Work, and you say you are so grateful, why don't you work?'

"I have been in the Work for thirty years, but I saw that I have never worked, certainly not as I now understand working."

He sat there with tears in his eyes. It was clear that he was deeply touched by her remark.

I left Paris a few days later. Soon after, I heard that my friend had died. I was sure that he had escaped the possibility of the torments of Hell and that he was certainly enjoying the pleasures of Paradise. But I wondered if his deepest wish, which he was beginning to discover only towards the end of his life, was going to be granted to him. He wanted to be responsible, and wished to lessen the sorrow of His Endlessness. I wondered if he would have the courage and the guidance to forego the pleasures of Paradise and ask for a sojourn in Purgatory where he might work and learn to be responsible.

Dikran had himself often talked like this, in those very words. I wondered whether I would have the opportunity to choose. What would I choose: Paradise or Purgatory?

Paris, 1989.

Something That Does Not Die

O n this fortieth anniversary of Gurdjieff's death, I wish to understand a remark of Madame de Salzmann's that unless one can die intentionally one cannot live intentionally. How can I understand this? More importantly, how can I practice it? It can hardly be a matter of a rational comprehension or analysis. Above all, I need to practice this dying in quiet work.

❖ ❖ ❖

I came to New York yesterday as part of my annual ritual. Madame de Salzmann seems to have aged considerably in the past year; she is nearly a hundred and one. Still, she was very strong in the senior group meeting. She much emphasized the fact that it is very difficult to make a connection with the higher energy. With work, especially with others, one can make this connection for a few brief moments. That itself will reveal what is to be done. This connection is necessary, and even a little of it is very useful.

I said that sometimes I am surprised by what I say in the groups and even at the university and in public lectures. When I work by myself I am always in my way, and assertions of the ego, tensions and reactions are constantly there. But I can be a relatively purer channel if either someone else is in charge or if someone else asks a question of me and needs help. I was in the middle of a sentence when suddenly she said, "Stop!" She was very strong. My right hand was raised. I tried to keep my posture, gesture, attitude, as they were, as in the Stop exercise, without moving.

It was one of the most direct instructions that I have received from her. I had a very intense and direct impression of myself.

One of the particularly striking features of Madame de Salzmann's being seems to be that, in her presence, one can be clearly mindful of one's nothingness and suffer for it, but one does not feel reduced. There is nothing personal when she makes us aware of our nullity. What she helps one see is the human situation. In her presence there is always hope and one is drawn to the possibility of undertaking something serious and worthy of a real human being.

❖ ❖ ❖

When I met Madame de Salzmann, she was very distant and withdrawn. That intense and penetrating attention which has been her hallmark was not there. She asked me whether I play the piano. She was surprised that I do not play. She said, "You used to do something, and I saw you very often." I told her that I did meet her very often in the past and worked with her, and that we sometimes spoke about Krishnamurti.

I again asked her what I had asked at the group meeting. It seems that I can be more easily a conduit as a student or as a teacher, but not so much by myself. I need someone else, in a vertical line, for me to be available to a higher presence. She said, "I know that very well."

Again she withdrew into herself. After some time she said, *"Parlez d'autre choses."* ("Speak of other things.")

I asked, "Do you sense the other side of death?" I had to translate this into French before she understood my question.

"Yes, of course; very clearly." But then she would not say anything else about it. After a little while she said, "I get into different states, very high states, and that shows me many things."

Suddenly, she asked, *"Qu'est-ce que vous voulez? Qu'est-ce qu'on va faire?"* ("What do you wish? What is one going to do?")

I said, "*Il faut servir quelque chose en haut.*" ("One must serve something higher.")

"*Se servir de quelque chose ou servir quelque chose?*" she demanded. ("To be served by something or to serve something?")

"*Servir quelque chose. Mais je vois la difficulté. Je n'ai pas la connaisance ou l'attention solide.*" ("To serve something. But I see the difficulty. I do not have the knowledge or steady attention.")

When leaving, I took both of her hands in mine. Since she was sitting on the sofa, I kneeled on the floor, holding her hands, my hands in front of me as in the Indian greeting. I said, "*Je sens que je suis en Inde,*" ("I feel I am in India") and a thought flashed through my mind that I should touch her feet as one would in India. She gave me a very warm smile.

❖ ❖ ❖

On another occasion, when I arrived to see Madame de Salzmann she was watching a video of the Movements. The large scale version of a Movements film had been reduced to a video size and this distorted and elongated the people in the film. I sat and watched the remainder of the video with her. She said after the video was finished, "That was another moment. Very different."

I wondered if those who had worked with her intensely on the Movements had understood something real about the Movements. She said, "They don't realize how difficult it is to do the Movements rightly."

I wondered if she was satisfied with the Movements in the latest film. "I cannot say I am satisfied." Then she was quiet and pensive for a while.

I asked if there is anything that continues after death. "That depends. Not for everyone. But if one works one can develop something that does not die at the death of the body." Again, she was quiet, in-drawn.

After a little while she asked me, "What do you do? How do you work? What interests you?"

I said I try to make a contact between the mind and the body, and that sometimes I have a strong sensation in my back. But, in general, I do not have a firm enough connection. "What I wish for is knowledge that is solid and substantial, something I can touch and taste, even eat. Not just mental knowledge."

Madame de Salzmann was very interested, and for a little while really engaged with me. After some time she repeated again that it is necessary to see how difficult the work is. Then she asked, "What interests you in life?"

I said that sacred words (I said '*les mots sacrés*' because I was not sure of the French word for 'scripture') such as the Gospels and the *Bhagavad Gita* interested me. I said that sometimes I am very moved by them. "I understand that very well," she said.

She was in no hurry for me to go, but after about an hour I decided to leave. When I got up to take my leave, she wondered if I was going far and for long. I said, yes. She insisted on getting up from her sofa and walking with me to the elevator. More than once she said we should be together soon. "I hope you will come to see me soon. *Monsieur, c'est necessaire d'être ensemble.* (It is necessary to be together.) When will I see you again?"

I said, "Perhaps in a few months. In Paris."

"Oh, that is too long. It may be too late. Come soon. I have many things here," she said pointing to her head, "which I need to tell you."

The elevator came and she stood there waving to me. "*Merci! Au revoir, monsieur.*" I too said, "*Au revoir,*" and was glad that the elevator doors closed, for I had tears in my eyes. I am clearly a member of her family. Her image, externally frail but full of inner force, saying 'thank you' to me and waving good-bye, engraved itself in my heart.

I felt a strong sense of gratitude, towards her and towards the Work. For the first time I understood the words of St. Paul, "A necessity is laid upon my soul; woe is unto me if I do not preach the gospel." Having seen Madame de Salzmann and having been instructed by her leaves one no choice: one is obliged to work.

Halifax, October 1989; New York, December 1989.

The Evolution of Higher Energy

M adame de Salzmann is gravely ill, and Michel and Josée are very occupied with that. Madame de Dampierre said this is not the time for private meetings. It seems that Madame de Salzmann is unable to speak. Last December in New York I had been fairly certain that my meetings with Madame de Salzmann were over. I am left with a strong image of her waving goodbye, inviting me to come and see her soon, pointing to her head and saying that she had many things in there which she would like to tell me.

This evening, Madame de Salzmann's group, to which I used to go, met and sat working completely quietly for forty-five minutes. Then everybody left. I found it very interesting and touching; the group has matured a lot. I kept wondering what I could do for Madame de Salzmann. I wonder if I could arrange to sit next to her and hold her hand.

❖ ❖ ❖

During the work Sunday at the Maison, I was asked to go through a volume of material gathered by the California group for the *Gurdjieff Annotated Bibliography*. Some of the material is fascinating, including several pictures from the twenties. Apparently, in November 1915 the notice in the *Voice of Moscow* spoke about the Indian mystery play, "The Struggle of the Magicians," by G. Gurdjieff, a Hindu! Also, de Hartmann composed and conducted the music for an opera by

Rabindranath Tagore, "The King of the Dark Room." (I had read this in India many years ago as "The King of the Dark Chamber.")

I had written a note for Michel that I would like to say my farewell to Madame de Salzmann. Even without looking at my note, he said, "Of course, you must see her. It is important." He seems completely convinced that the end is near. It could be any day; certainly he would be surprised if she survives this year. He spoke about the ending of an epoch in the Work, the first epoch being when Gurdjieff was alive, and the second one with his mother. I went to the de Salzmann house at four o'clock to see Madame de Salzmann. There was such a strong atmosphere of farewell in the place, a sombre and serious witnessing of a great transition.

Michel announced my name to Madame de Salzmann. I could hear all this from the adjoining room. Of course, she did not know who I was. He repeated my name a few times, and said, "*l'Indien.*" I did not hear clearly what she said. In any case, he ushered me in, saying that I should speak loudly for she is hard of hearing. I entered with hands folded *à l'Indien.* She said in French, "How are you?" Michel said to her that I prefer to speak in English. I protested and said she could speak in French. Michel went out of the room and left me alone with her.

Madame de Salzmann said with a smile that she could speak English. But then she continued in French, "*Je peux parler en anglais.*" She again asked me how I was. I said, "I am fine but you don't look well." She agreed.

I reminded her that when I last saw her in New York she had said pointing to her head, "I have many things in here which I wish to tell you."

"Was that good?" she asked.

She was obviously in pain. When a stab of pain occurred, her whole face changed as if it were a mask that was perturbed, leaving her essential being quite untouched. A part of me would rather not have seen her at all in her present situation, but it is necessary to see and understand the laws to which the body is subject. All the great spiritual traditions say that the real person is not the body. What is expressed as a great hope in these traditions was manifestly visible as a fact in the case of Madame de Salzmann. She herself had so often said, "The body must obey something higher, otherwise it has no purpose. It cannot serve only itself. The body itself is designed for destruction, but it can serve something else."

I recalled what she had said several years earlier: "There is an energy which is trying to evolve. That is why it comes into a body. If a person works and helps the evolution of this energy, at death this energy goes to a higher level. Energies of different qualities have different durations. The energy of a higher level does not die at the death of a lower level. The higher energy is in the body, but it is not of the body."

There can be no question that there has been a great evolution of the higher energy which incarnated in her. I wonder where she is heading now. I suspect she will be one of the 'All-Quarters-Maintainers'. God bless her!

When it was time for me to go, I said, "I must say 'farewell' and ask for your blessing." She smiled and held my hand. I left with moist eyes. Although it is right and timely for her to go, I will miss her. One cannot but wonder with the Psalmist, "What is man that thou art mindful of him?"

❖ ❖ ❖

Next morning, I woke up recalling, for no reason that I know, the Vedic sage Uddalka asking his son Shvetaketu Aruneya, "Now that you are so learned in many sciences, and so full of yourself, have you learned how to hear the unhearable? And how to see the invisible?"

Something, deep down in me, responded with an echo of the *Rig Veda*, "There is many a dawn which has not yet risen."

Paris, April 1990.

There Is Many a Dawn Which Has Not Yet Risen

Madame de Dampierre said to me, "Very few people, perhaps only two or three, understood what Madame de Salzmann was trying to bring, and how difficult it is. To realize that what I do is not enough, not quite yet, is the only way for me to keep the inner work alive. It is important to keep struggling with the body, by denying something, by fasting, or other things." At the end of our meeting she said, "It is clear that Madame de Salzmann gave you a lot. When you came in the beginning, she had spoken to me to take care of you."

It seems entirely clear that the cosmos is not here for me, and that the Gurdjieff Work is not here for me. To the extent the Work serves something objective and true, the only interest it can have in me is in preparing me to serve something objective and true. If the Work is used to serve my ego, or business or pleasure, then the teachers in the Work have failed in their mission and work, or I have failed them, at least with respect to this incarnation. Why would a remarkable person like Madame de Salzmann spend time and energy on me? For her pleasure? For mine? I need to remember what happens to the pullets which do not lay eggs.

How will I pay my debt to the Gurdjieff Teaching? How can I really serve? Above all, by working, so that the only thing needful would be done, namely, to be pervaded by the Spirit. At some stage in one's life a serious person has to be able to say, "I do not require any more honour, money or pleasure; I have what I need." I must constantly ask: "What is the one thing needful to do so that this incarnation is not wasted?"

❖ ❖ ❖

My meetings with Michel seem to be fated and necessary, and they almost always have a sense of profundity. When I met him I told him that all eyes are on him. This is hardly news to him. He responded without a trace of vanity, and with an amazing amount of openness. He said, "I am not a group leader, because I have no groups of my own." Whatever he means by it, I am sure he feels he is carrying out the wishes, instructions and the work of his teacher, who is also his mother, and therefore that he does not have any groups of his own. Of course, he has to find his own style, his own words and emphasis, even though the essential work is the same. This was also true for Madame de Salzmann who was truly original, neither novel nor imitative.

Michel said that *kaliyuga* (one of the four divisions, the one we are in and the worst one, of a great cycle of time in Indian cosmology) and such other concepts may be speaking of realities which are internal and present all the time. He also said that a teacher is one who can bow to something above herself. Thus the teacher evokes a natural respect.

It is clear that Michel is obliged to undertake a great *yajña*. It will not be easy. I felt much friendship and affection for him and gave him a book with an inscription to that effect. I told him that I know he has a difficult task. I wish to help anyway that I can. I said, "I feel like your brother." I am sure that spiritual kinship has more significance and lasts longer than biological kinship.

❖ ❖ ❖

In an unusually strong meditation sitting at the Maison, I experienced such a sense of substantial connection above the head, almost a pressure of presence and yet a lightness. At the end of the sitting, Michel gave the news about Madame de Salzmann. He specifically mentioned the remark I had made to him a few days earlier at his home that we are all members of Madame de Salzmann's family. He said, "I wish to tell you directly about her news. She has cancer of the bladder for which she had surgery two years ago in New York, and the cancer is now spreading. She recently had surgery again, mainly to remove some pain. She is back home, and it may be possible for some groups to see her, perhaps in the Fall. She had, one day, especially spoken to me very much as if from the other shore and regretted her inability to work with us." Then he spoke of other things. He was not at all sentimental or anxious, simply matter of fact.

❖ ❖ ❖

The visit to Paris is over. Madame de Salzmann is dying. For the Work an era is ending. No doubt there will be a new dawn. Almost certainly Michel will be an important and bright light in the new sky, but it remains to be seen what light and what colors will shine.

For me, too, an era is ending. The only people who have been in the position of teachers for me have been Krishnamurti, Madame de Salzmann and Mrs. Welch. Krishnamurti has been gone for a few years; Madame de Salzmann's departure is imminent; and Mrs. Welch has not been a teacher for me since the early eighties, for she had chosen to become a senior advisor and colleague after I started working with Madame de Salzmann. There are some associates and fellow travelers here and there, and some students. So much is needed, so little is understood. Lord, have mercy.

❖ ❖ ❖

Madame de Salzmann died yesterday. Her era has now ended. The whole older generation is fast disappearing. The teachers connect us with the source; they create demands and gauge our understanding. Now, how do we truly stand in the line of transmission?

On hearing the news of her death, my wife and I sat quietly together. Some feeling overwhelmed me and I wept uncontrollably for a few minutes. Soon, arrangements and many phone calls had to be made. I was hesitant to go to Paris for the final rites of Madame de Salzmann. I am tired of traveling, I came back from Paris only eight days ago, and it is expensive. But I cannot not go. Madame de Salzmann has been my teacher, especially for the last ten years. She was indefatigably generous to me, with her time, energy and attention. Whatever I understand about the work is mainly a result of my work with her. I am obliged to obey what she obeyed. I have to go to Paris. Furthermore, the Welches cannot go; nor is anyone else going from the Welch groups.

We had an extraordinary gathering in the Work House in Halifax, from six o'clock to midnight, alternating between meditation sittings, readings, the Movements and music. Various people who had met Madame de Salzmann spoke about their early and later impressions of her. It was good to work for clarity of feeling: it was not the occasion for regret or unhappiness, but more for gratitude and a renewal of a contact with what calls. The whole extraordinary evening was rich, quiet and deep.

Late in the evening I phoned the Welches. I felt that they needed to be supported, even more than the rest of us. After all, we can still look to them and phone them for wise counsel. Who could they call upon now? Who is their teacher now? Or who can be an elder for them? I read to them the entry of December 1988 in which Madame de Salzmann had asked, "If God were here close to you and He does not touch you, or at least you think He does not touch you, how would you invite Him to touch you? How would you open to Him?" They were both very moved.

I woke up this morning with some words spoken by Madame de Salzmann still ringing in my ears, words which I had never heard her actually say: "I see that oneself is a part of all; and all is a part of one."

I wonder in which world, in what form, she is now going to work. I again recalled the confident affirmation of the *Rig Veda* which, in its whispering of objective hope, reminds me of so many remarks of Madame de Salzmann, "There is many a dawn which has not yet risen."

❖ ❖ ❖

I have just come from sitting near Madame de Salzmann. When I entered, I instinctively folded my hands to the body, saluting and greeting in the Indian style. In solemn moments I seem to return to a deep physical memory of my essential upbringing in India. Madame de Salzmann had an extraordinary presence, even in death. It seemed as if she would speak any moment. In between, I almost glimpsed her lips move.

During the time I sat near Madame de Salzmann's body many things flashed through my mind. I remembered many moments with her. My first major meeting with her, when I arrived so late and she had said, "It is important not to give in to reaction." And later meetings when she said, "Did you help?"; "It cannot not be the case that nobody is without no use"; "You remind me of myself when I was young— determined, and arrogant." I remembered going with her to Gurdjieff's apartment, and the time when she insisted that I should have her private number in England when she was away in case I needed to reach her, and so on. So many major insights in my life, so many moments of deep feeling, have taken place during meetings with her. Now I was here to say goodbye and farewell.

I left the room after about an hour, and spoke to Michel for a few minutes. He gave me coffee and I told him that Dr. Welch wanted me to tell him what the groups had undertaken in New York, Toronto, Halifax and other places, and also why the Welches could not come. Michel was clearly happy that I had come. He wondered if I was there when he had spoken to the group at the Maison a couple of weeks ago about us being in the family of Madame de Salzmann. He told me that he has not slept very much for the last two months. One night he got up to get his son from the airport and fell on all fours out of dizziness. He certainly wants to conquer his body, and he will probably succeed, if anyone can.

I had told Michel that one of the unexpected thoughts which had flashed through my mind while sitting close to Madame de Salzmann was that having met in her the best the West has to offer, now I could go back to India. Strange! He thought that in my dream I imagine that the whole world is one, but there are different influences. I do not think I quite heard what he said. In any case, I did not know what he meant.

Before leaving, I went in to see Madame de Salzmann again. This time, I sat on the other side, which was better lit. I sat for half an hour or so. I offered gratitude and farewell to Madame de Salzmann on behalf of the Welches, my wife and our group. There was an extraordinary presence in the room. She had a stern look, as stern on herself as it was demanding of others. It seemed as if she could speak at any moment. I had convinced myself in group meetings with her that she would not refuse to be engaged if I asked a question and continued to smile. I wondered if this trick would work now. I smiled, more internally than outwardly, and felt that she smiled back and said, "Yes!"

❖ ❖ ❖

I have just come back from the religious service in the Russian church in Paris, the St. Alexandre Nevsky, at 12 *rue Daru*. The solemn gathering of perhaps two hundred and fifty people, mostly French and English and a few Americans, could hardly not be touching. There was respect and silence. Outside the church, Michel embraced me. He has much on his shoulders I felt for him deeply and said, "God bless you!"

One epoch is now ended, perhaps for the world, for the Work certainly, and for me personally. What a remarkable teacher Madame de Salzmann has been! All those who came in contact with her are blessed. She was like a mountain resonating only to the objectively corresponding vibrations of search for connection with higher energy. At the same time she embodied a heart without measure. All those who were her pupils have in their memory her impartial and objective look, issuing a strong call. Not to respond is to waste this incarnation.

God bless you, Madame de Salzmann, in whichever world you are now working!

Paris, May 1990; Halifax, May 1990.

Remarks of Madame de Salzmann

Why Are You on the Earth?

It is not important how long one lives, but whether one develops something which can give meaning to life. What do you wish in life? Why are you on the Earth?

❖

If God were here close to you and He does not touch you, or at least you think He does not touch you, how would you invite Him to touch you? How would you open to Him?

❖

The body must obey something higher, otherwise it has no purpose. It cannot serve only itself. The body itself is designed for destruction, but it can serve something else.

❖

Energies of different qualities have different durations. The energy of a higher level does not die at the death of a lower level. The higher energy is in the body, but it is not of the body.

❖

Epilogue

For a long time after Madame de Salzmann's death I felt bereaved and listless, as if my lover had died. Then I felt a strong need to consolidate my understanding of her instructions in the work, and I wished to stay with facts as she had defined them: "What you know directly is a fact."

Perhaps partly owing to my Indian cultural background in which the contact with and instruction from a living teacher is much more important than any books, institutions or doctrines, for me the specificity of the Work is constituted more by Madame de Salzmann, and less by any particular idea or practice. Gurdjieff himself constituted the specificity of the Work for those for whom he was the teacher. In spite of the public nature of the massive and outstanding body of ideas, music and sacred dances associated with the Gurdjieff teaching, the Work is fundamentally an esoteric and oral tradition. The essential teaching takes place from a teacher to a pupil. The meaning and practice of the Work are understood in the direct contact and exchange between those who have clarity about the undertaking as well as compassion for the human situation and those who wish to understand the human possibility and responsibility.

Of course, every worthy teacher is also a student, wishing to listen to and obey a higher authority. Only such a person can make a demand and offer hope, without evoking ego reactions or sentimental adulation. It is also true that strictly speaking there is no meaning to a spiritual lineage or an initiation which is given to one person by another. All true initiation is Self-initiation, from the Source. Teachers simply point the way. In the presence of the vibration of Truth, there is no difference between a teacher and a student. Even as great a teacher as Jesus Christ did not wish to claim any special status for himself and said, "Why call me good? No one is good but God."

The Gospels say it, and it must be true, that from those to whom much is given much is demanded. Without doubt, I have been given much, and sometimes I clearly understand the need for payment. As

Madame de Salzmann said, the real payment is made only by working. I know in my conscience that what I bring to this is not enough. But one needs to begin again and again. I once asked Madame de Salzmann how to make efforts in the Work without fear. She had said, "The real fear is the fear of 'not being able to'." I wish to pay for my existence; not to be able to pay is terrifying. But a recognition of the terror of the situation is necessary in order to work for being and for being able to.

Like everyone else, I must at some stage give an account of my life. For me the clear objective conscience, the look from above, is personified by Madame de Salzmann. At the end of my days, at the time of reckoning, I do not expect Madame de Salzmann to ask whether or not I succeeded in what I undertook in the name of the Work. She is likely to ask, "Did you help?"

On many occasions, especially in quiet work, I have felt a strong presence of Madame de Salzmann, inside me and nearby. She always has that characteristically subtle combination of a stern and a compassionate look, demanding and encouraging. In those moments it seems quite clear that the work is objective. It is not her work or my work. It is something which is objectively needed and without which our world cannot be maintained. The heart of the work is a continual sacrificing of the merely personal for the sake of the Real. Only that sacrifice permits an exchange with higher levels. Also, of course, an exchange with higher levels makes the sacrifice of the personal meaningful. A sage in the *Rig Veda* has truly said that "*yajña* ('sacrifice' as well as 'exchange between levels') is the navel of the cosmos."

The whole cosmos is engaged in a ceaseless *yajña*. Sacred work, which in alchemical language, as in the Gurdjieff teaching, is simply spoken of as the work, is necessary in order to be able to receive energy from above for the maintenance of the cosmos, both on the scale of an individual human being and on the large scale. But it is constantly threatened by the forces of forgetfulness and destruction. One deviates continually from the freedom of the work, which comes only when one is connected with higher energy, and returns to fear and self-importance. A repeated returning to a state of self-remembering, a recovery of the connection with the Real, is needed in order to fulfill the purpose of one's incarnation on the Earth.

Madame de Salzmann said, "Man has a special function, which other creatures cannot fulfill. He can serve the Earth by becoming a bridge for certain higher energies. Without this the Earth cannot live properly. But man, as he is by nature, is not complete. In order to fulfill his proper function he needs to develop. There is a part in him which is unsatisfied by his life. Through religious or spiritual traditions he may become aware of what this part needs."

How do we play our part in fulfilling the special human function in the cosmos?

Epilogue to the Second Edition

The major event in the Work since the publication of *Heart Without Measure* almost five years ago has been the passing away of Dr. Michel de Salzmann. His enormous contribution to the Work became even more obvious with the large gap left by his absence. Although he had wanted to write a preface for the hardcover edition, he had not been able to do so owing to ill health. He was keen to see *Heart Without Measure* in paperback and had planned to write a preface for it. I would like to take the occasion of the publication of this edition to express my gratitude to him.

Michel de Salzmann had taken much interest in the preparation of *Heart Without Measure*. After some exchange of notes, he came to Nova Scotia for a weekend explicitly to work on the manuscript. Soon afterwards, I went to Paris and stayed with him for a week and we spent most of our time and energy working on it. Michel read every word of the manuscript and made many useful suggestions. At one point he said to me with much warmth, "You give me a different picture of my own mother."

Michel was an entirely remarkable man. I am proud to have worked with him and to have been considered a friend by him. Madame de Salzmann had said several times, and in different ways, that Michel and I will understand each other. After Michel's death, sitting in the room where his body lay, I was very struck by the expression of inquiry on his face. Even in the stillness of death, I felt his continuing search for the essential. He never spared himself, nor anyone else who worked with him. I had no doubt that his search was continuing in other realms.

In his bedroom, on the wall facing him, was a photograph of Ramana Maharishi whom he much admired and who made the inquiry 'Who am I?' the cornerstone of the spiritual work for all his pupils. Also, there were two framed verses from the *Bhagavad Gita* with both the Sanskrit original and the translation in French in calligraphy. One of them speaks as directly of Michel as anything else:

Involved, but not identified,
The various forces of nature do not disturb him.
He knows that this is all a play of forces.
He is firm, unshaken.